WE HAVE A WINNER!

We Have a Winner!

America's

WEIRD AND WONDERFUL RACES, DERBIES, PAGEANTS, AND EATING CONTESTS

RAILEY JANE SAVAGE

GUILFORD, CONNECTICUT

An imprint of Globe Pequot

Distributed by NATIONAL BOOK NETWORK

British Library Cataloguing in Publication Information available

Library of Congress Cataloging-in-Publication Data available

ISBN 978-1-4930-2904-4 (paperback)

ISBN 978-1-4930-2905-1 (e-book)

∞™ The paper used in this publication meets the minimum requirements of American National Standard for Information Sciences—Permanence of Paper for Printed Library Materials, ANSI/NISO Z39.48-1992.

Printed in the United States of America

FOR MY FAM DAMILY

MOM

TIM

CLARA

JACK

GRENDEL

AN EMBARRASSMENT OF WINNERS.

CONTENTS

INTRODUCTION 14

ON YOUR MARKS 18

Boom Run 20

Lawn Mower Racing 22

The Great Bunion Derby 24

Bed Racing 26

Six Day Bicycle Races 28

Shovel Racing 30

Joggling 32

24 Hours of LeMons 34

Outhouse Racing 36

Redneck Blank, Pig Roast and Music Festival 38

HERE SHE IS . . . 40

Miss America 42

Harvest Queen 44

Miss Unsafe Brakes 46

Miss'd America 48

Miss Klingon Empire 50

QUESTIONABLE FUN AND ESTEEMED TITLES 52

Mr. Mosquito Legs 54

Little Mr. Chaos and Miss Miscellaneous 56

The Hatfield McCoy Marathon & the Tug Fork Tug of War 58

World Pillow Fight Championship 60

Coffin Race Championship 62

Worm Gruntin' Championship 64

Disc Golf Championship 66

The Undie 500 68

FESTS AND CONTESTS 70

Bubble Gum Blowing 72

Kcymaerxthaere Spelling Bee 74

Moo-la-Palooza 76

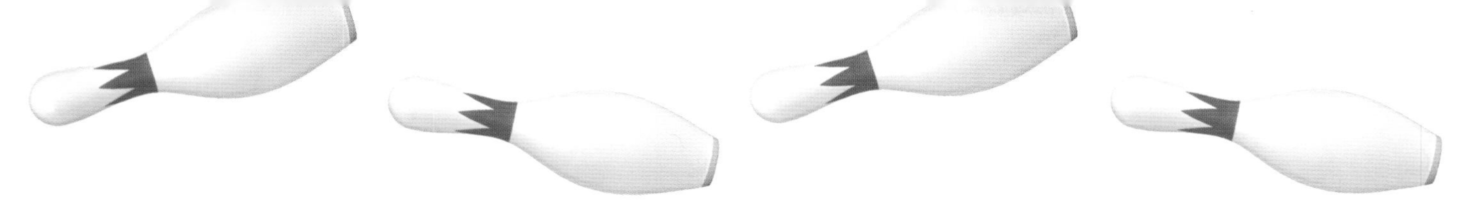

Rotten Sneaker Contest 78

Super Farmer Contest 80

The Great Salt Lick Contest 82

Milk Chugging Contest 84

Mom and Husband Calling 86

Ladies' Rubber Chicken Throwing Contest 88

Decorated Diaper Contest and Diaper Derby 90

DERBY, OR NOT DERBY? 92

Dole Air Derby 94

All-American Soap Box Derby 96

Father's Day Fishing Derby 98

All-American Dog Derby 100

The Kentucky Derby 102

Roller Derby 104

Demolition Derbies and Destructive Motorsports 106

Alvin "Shipwreck" Kelly dunking doughnuts in his native habitat—from atop a flagpole, 1939.

NO THANKS, I'M STUFFED! 108

Goldfish Swallowing 110

Pie Eating Contests 112

Nathan's Famous Hot Dog Eating Contest 114

The Manhattan Fat Men's Club 116

Alferd Packer Day Snacker Contest 118

MoonPie Eating Contests 120

Cupcake Chomping Contests 122

La Costeña Feel the Heat Jalapeño Eating Contest 124

The Ill-advised, the Unconventional, and the Unfortunate 126

BECAUSE, WHY NOT? 128

Phone Booth Stuffing 130

Flagpole Sitting 132

Kissing Contests 134

Rock, Paper, Scissors! 136

Ugly Lamp Contest 138

Ugly Dog Contest 140

Horse Soccer 142

Turkey Bowling 144

Most Gifted Wrapper 146

Duct Tape Prom Dresses! 148

HARDER, BETTER, FASTER, STRONGER 150

Venus de Milo Lookalike 152

Livestock Showcase 154

Agricultural Royalty 156

America's Giant Produce! 158

Bingo (Cow Chip, or Chicken) 160

Watermelon Pitted Against Watermelon 162

The Mystic Krewe of Barkus 164

POTLUCK! 166

Morel Pole—National Morel Mushroom Festival 168

Great Garlic Cook-Off—Gilroy Garlic Festival 170

Frog Leg Festival 172

Blue Ribbon Cricket Eating Contest 174

Cabbage Bowling, Toss, Decorating, Beer—Sauerkraut Weekend 176

West Virginia Roadkill Cook-Off & Autumn Harvest Festival 178

Great Potato Cook-Off—Barnesville Potato Days 180

Fluff Cooking Contest—What the Fluff? Festival 182

STAYING POWER 184

Hunkerin' 186

Rocking Chair Derbies 188

Hands on a Hardbody 190

Noun and Verb Rodeo 192

Dance Marathons 194

Dance Marathons *(Continued)* 196

Dance Marathons *(and Continued!)* 198

ACKNOWLEDGMENTS 202

PHOTO CREDITS 206

INDEX 216

ABOUT THE AUTHOR 222

DOUGHNUTS
BUY ONE

GROW IT YOURSELF
PLAN A FARM GARDEN NOW
DELTA COUNTY FAIR
HOTCHKISS COLORADO
FIRST PREMIUM
DELTA COUNTY FAIR

INTRODUCTION

When I was a young girl, I would spend hours with my grandmother watching movies. Once I was over my *Meet Me in St. Louis* phase, we moved on to *The Egg and I*, a now all-but-forgotten Claudette Colbert/Fred MacMurray comedy from the 1940s. A socialite and a New York exec quit their big-city lifestyle and move to a rundown chicken farm upstate. Hilarity and tribulations ensue. One thorn in their side is the pair of loud, uncouth, and unkempt neighbors, Ma and Pa Kettle. The Kettles went on to have their own film franchise of misdeeds and merriment, but were initially the loudest of the Greek chorus in *The*

The dance event at this pageant sponsored by the Dominicans of New Jersey brings the pink-clad beauties to the catwalk to strut their stuff.

Egg and I. While I loved the poultry hijinks and fish-out-of-water trouble the beautifully lithe Claudette found herself in, I was especially drawn to a scene at the county fair (not unlike the scenes at the World's Fair in *Meet Me in St. Louis*, in retrospect). People were happy, awestruck by the sights and sounds, and overwhelmed with pride when they won prizes in various competitions. Ma Kettle's quilt was an award winner, and Marjorie Main's face beamed. I could also see this pride in Scarlett O'Hara as she boasted having the smallest waist (seventeen inches) in the county. Or when Carl Denham presented King Kong, the largest ape anyone in America had ever seen. Or when Mr. Smith was a champion on the senate floor, filibustering for longer than anyone dared expect.

Eat up, boys.

The films were all old, but the sentiments still applied. There was an innately competitive nature in these iconic American characters, and their victories resonated with audiences of their time—and found new footing in an eight-year-old

A good ol' fashioned greased pig chase!

High-school beauty contest winners and Howdy the Rodeo mascot.

in the mid-1990s. The victories they celebrated ranged from the mundane to the miraculous, and yet each of them made me stand up and cheer. No matter the circumstances, I related to the desire and action to be the best at something.

These films are a reflection of the cultures in which they were produced, yet across the varied plot landscapes and the fifty-plus years between their production and my viewing them, these Americans all sought to be winners. The historic events over the past 150 years confirm that the fictional characters' reveling in being "the best" was true to form: Americans like to win. What is at least equally—if not more!—pertinent is the fact that it doesn't seem to matter what it is that we're the best at. Americans will find a platform on which to shine, even if we have to invent it.

So let's explore the various and wacky ways we Americans have found to declare ourselves winners. They are fantastic and often hilarious. Indeed, being the cabbage bowling champ, or the winner of the outhouse derby, or the mashed potato wrestling champ are titles only held by Americans (maybe because we are the only ones both wacky and competitive enough to claim these titles, and proudly).

But our embrace of the winner's circle, even if it is more in the tradition of *The Gong Show* than the Olympics, is unique, and well worth celebrating. Gusto, and documentation—photo finishes, as it were—have given this author plenty to work with. And yet, at the end of the day, all absurdity aside, the pride of being the best that shines in the winners' eyes continues to reflect in my own.

WHAT IS THE LARGEST COUNTY FAIR IN THE UNITED STATES?

The Erie County Fair is held in Hamburg in Erie County, New York, every August. Based on 2014 attendance, it is the largest fair in New York and the third-largest county fair in the United States, often drawing over 1 million in attendance. But the crown goes to the San Diego County Fair, which saw attendance of 1.5 million in 2014.

ON YOUR MARKS

BEING THE FASTEST IS GOOD. Being the fastest at something unique and wildly impractical is better. Rather than settling for a competition of innate and cultivated human speed, Americans have a history of upping the ante by adding other elements to races: You can run fast, but can you run fast across floating logs? You can build a fast car, but can you build a fast bed? The impracticality of these competitions is celebrated, precisely because they are so wacky and demanding in unique ways—if you create a niche market, you are much more likely to corner, and conquer, it.

BOOM RUN

LAWN MOWER RACING

THE GREAT BUNION DERBY

BED RACING

SIX DAY BICYCLE RACES

SHOVEL RACING

JOGGLING

24 HOURS OF LEMONS

OUTHOUSE RACING

REDNECK BLANK, PIG ROAST AND MUSIC FESTIVAL

BOOM RUN

HAYWARD, WISCONSIN, is home to the Lumberjack World Championships, a collection of games and competitions celebrating America's long history in the logging industry. The championships have been held annually since 1960 and now draw thousands of visitors to a town with a population of just over 2,000. There can be no question of America's fervor for logging in the nineteenth and early twentieth centuries, and the unique skills the industry demanded are tested through the championships. In addition to pole climbing, log rolling, and the ever-popular chainsaw events, the boom run is an event that commands increasingly enthusiastic crowds—particularly the women's contests. In the boom run a series of logs are chained end to end and stretched across a pond. The competitors have to run across them, touch a marker, then run back to the starting point. The fastest (not necessarily the driest) is the winner. This event tests competitors on the racing triumvirate—speed, balance, and agility—but with the added wrinkle of field testing who has the best water-resistant footwear.

Leaping from log to log, she runs to find victory at the Midwest Log Rolling Championships in Madison, Wisconsin.

ALSO HAPPENING

In 1960, when the first Boom Run championships were held, here's what else was happening:

MOST POPULAR MOVIES: *The Bridge on the River Kwai* and *The Ten Commandments.*

CELEBRITIES: Elvis Presley, Rock Hudson, Kim Novac.

AROUND THE WORLD: Laika the dog launched into space aboard Sputnik II.

FADS!: Slinkys and hula hoops.

LAWN MOWER RACING

LADIES AND GENTLEMEN, PRIME YOUR ENGINES.

Americans have applied their souped-up, bigger-is-better, I-can-beat-everyone attitudes and efforts to some of the most utilitarian things in their lives—in this case, their lawn mowers. Though ride-on mowers are a British invention, further refined by the Australians, racing them was first made popular in Twelve Mile, Indiana, in 1963 with the Twelve Mile 500 (à la the more famous, higher-speed car race held in Indianapolis every year). In 1992 the USLMRA, or the United States Lawn Mower Racing Association, was founded as the official governing body of yard-equipment-based races in North America. With its slogan, "The MOW the Merrier," it holds races all over the country each year as people remove the blades from their rigs and take off around carefully constructed—though ironically, usually grass-free—racetracks in hopes of bringing glory and bragging rights to their home turf. Why not turn everything we own into a competitive tool? After all, the MOW the merrier.

They may not be mowing, but these machines are put to the test, and only the best can have his day in the sun (or dirt).

PRE-MOWER MAINTENANCE

The lawn mower was invented in 1830 as an improvement on the scythe and for use on sports grounds or large gardens. The concept of a "lawn" was not popularized yet, as most people couldn't afford to keep a patch of land that was not used for agricultural purposes, and those who could afford to have ornamental swaths of grass might have had a small army of sheep, goats, and geese to take care of most of the excess grass.

THE GREAT BUNION DERBY

IN 1928, 199 RUNNERS LEFT LOS ANGELES to participate in America's first transcontinental race. Nearly three months later, fifty-five stalwart souls (soles?) arrived in New York City, finishing the 3,425-mile course. The race was the first of its kind and was organized by one C. C. Pyle, America's first sports agent. Baseball, football, tennis, and boxing were all in the throes of happy heydays, and "Cash and Carry" Pyle was quick to capitalize on America's thirst for athletic competitions. His race was so grueling that he was redubbed "Corns and Callouses" Pyle, and the press named the event the Bunion Derby. In addition to being the inaugural transcontinental footrace, the Bunion Derby is notable for its winner, Andy Payne, a twenty-year-old part-Cherokee boy, who won handily, and Ed Gardner, who came in eighth and, as a black man, helped give America a preview of what integrated athletic competition would look like. Alas, the Bunion Derby folded after its second year, though it paved the way for large-scale races, and running-based foot injuries, for future generations.

Andy Payne, who will go on to win the race, and a fellow runner jog out of Grand Canyon National Park in Williams, Arizona, 1928.

THE OPPOSITE OF RACING?

Records from stationary competition:

COMPETITIVE TELEVISION WATCHING: 72 hours watching while someone else controlled the remote.

COMPETITIVE SNAKE SITTING: 45 minutes in a bathtub with 87 rattlesnakes.

BED OF NAILS: 283 hours lying on a bed of nails.

COMPETITIVE INSTANT MESSAGING: 96 hours straight sitting at the computer, "socializing."

As if they really need the neon sign to let you know what you're getting into . . .

BED RACING

THOUGH BED RACING IS HISTORICALLY AND MOST FAMOUSLY BRITISH, there are American iterations that undoubtedly qualify as "wacky." Like any race, speed is key, though often hard to attain with a decidedly un-aerodynamic bed, so ingenuity and creativity are the keys to success. The "beds" are typically fitted with handles on the four posters so that four members of the five-person team can push the craft as swiftly as possible while the remaining member stays "in bed." The Great Bed Races of the Kentucky Derby Festival are competitive, indeed, in 2017 going into their nearly thirtieth year of over forty teams lusting after the unique title of Fastest Bed. The event features the silly and the serious: Over-the-top beds-on-wheels and garish costumes adorn athletic teams, all against the backdrop of the otherwise straight-laced Broadbent Arena. Other races around the country are more straightforwardly fun fare, as in Miami, Florida, where the interludes between heats feature musical performances, stand-up comedians, and celebrity judges. Just think: Your bed performance, too, could be judged by Vanilla Ice.

With tissue paper tiki torches aflame, a team competes in Southern Arkansas University's Family Day.

WATERBEDS

Bona fide waterbeds didn't rock the sleep industry until the late 1960s when things were groovy and hepcats were welcoming a little shake-up in the bedroom. The 1970s saw civil unrest in America, but the waterbed boom ensured that Americans were at least getting a good night's rest. The 1980s were all day-traders and discotheques, and waterbeds made sure that the witching hours had a welcome case of Night Fever. Come the 1990s, however, and that scene where Edward Scissorhands pierced his bed and officially scarred a generation, waterbeds managed to retain their buoyancy but lost their nighttime cachet.

SIX DAY BICYCLE RACES

FOUNDED IN 1891 THE SIX DAYS OF NEW YORK bicycle race remains the most famous of its kind. A wildly popular sport/spectacle in the first decades of the twentieth century, six-day races combined speed, endurance, and danger: Cyclists rode swiftly around a steeply banked indoor track, and the American public ate it up. The races were originally done solo—a single rider would complete as many laps around the track as he was able to within six days, sleeping when needed and spending the rest of his time on the bike. Riders suffered from exhaustion, hallucinations, and severe injuries, which prompted the State of New York to declare twelve consecutive hours to be the max a person could compete without a break. So in 1899, to maintain the thrill level and to get around certain safety precautions, two-man teams developed, allowing one member of each team to be cycling at any given time. Six Days of New York was held at Madison Square Garden and, at its peak, attracted over 20,000 spectators (including Bing Crosby and Barbara Stanwyck) who flocked to see the exhausted athletes push themselves to the limit, and then some. Teams could cycle well over 1,000 miles over the six-day period, and the standing world record was set in 1914 with two Australians logging nearly 2,760 miles.

The second iteration of Madison Square Garden (1925) was home to a variety of events but was built with bicycle racing in mind, and the huge track was home to all seventy-three editions of the historic, and notorious, Six Days of New York race.

Even when essentially empty, the velodromes from the turn of the twentieth century remain impressive; these cyclists used the free time and space to practice for a six-day race in about 1909.

SHOVEL RACING

1. ACQUIRE RUN-OF-THE-MILL GRAIN SHOVEL.
2. SIT ON SHOVEL.
3. SLIDE DOWN MOUNTAIN.

These are the founding—and only—principles of shovel racing. The snowy slopes of the southern Rockies at the Angel Fire Resort in New Mexico gave rise to this high-speed competition in the 1970s. By the 1990s competition had morphed into a battle of engineering with contestants modifying and customizing their shovels beyond recognition. With the growth of the sport came an increase in the odds that a fatal injury was going to put the sport six feet under, so the annual championships were suspended. They have since returned with the caveat that shovels cannot be modified beyond the addition of wax and paint. Even without modifications, riders can reach speeds of nearly seventy mph. At its apogee in the 1990s, shovel racing got a brief moment in the sun when it was an event at the 1997 ESPN Winter X Games, but super-modified shovel racing failed to catch on as a must-have winter event. The Angel Fire Resort continues to hold annual competitions, drawing enthusiasm from local veterans of the sport and bemused looks from Angel Fire guests.

Top: Outstanding form at the 2011 Shovel Races in Angel Fire, New Mexico.
Bottom: Not so outstanding form.

DIG DEEP

With the rise of agriculture came the shovel. From as early as the Stone Age (30,000 years ago) humans were using the shoulder bones of large animals to move dirt, stones, and materials. A 6,000-year-old sharpened elk antler tied to a piece of wood was found in a Russian bog, and it is thought to be the first snow shovel. Practically every laborer before 1900 spent an undue amount of time shoveling, yet it was only in conjunction with the excavator being introduced that shovels were designed for specific materials—snow, coal, grain, etc. The development of the shovel, however, has yet to eliminate the need for a back in back-breaking work.

JOGGLING

JUGGLING + JOGGING = JOGGLING

The International Jugglers' Association (IJA), the world's largest nonprofit circus organization, has held an annual festival in a different North American city since 1948. When in 1980 the man responsible for the IJA newsletter wanted to drum up interest in his preferred activity, he unleashed competitive joggling on the world. It took until 2008 to officially incorporate the World Joggling Championships into the IJA's annual festival, though.

There are various distance events, with varying numbers of balls. For the seven-ball events, competitors have to prove they can handle that number of "props" even without running; and for longer, five-ball events, competitors have to prove they can actually run (while juggling). Enthusiasts demonstrate a level of seriousness that belies the sport's young age and niche market. Outside the IJA festival and the annual juggling summit in Europe, jogglers grab their many balls and make appearances at foot races and marathons all over the country, though rarely in numbers greater than one.

Rumor has it he dropped the balls right after this photo was taken, but this joggler certainly looks determined at a race in Des Moines, Iowa, in 2010.

OTHER THINGS THAT SHOULDN'T GO TOGETHER

UNICYCLE FOOTBALL: Football, as in soccer, except on unicycles. Ouch.

EXTREME IRONING: Ironing using an ironing board in extreme circumstances, like surfing, snowboarding, and driving.

CHESS BOXING: One part brutality, two parts intellect.

UNDERWATER HOCKEY: Hit a ball into a goal. But do it underwater.

U.S. Coast Guard Academy Third Class Cadet Collin Sykes defends the puck from his opponents during an underwater hockey game at the University of Connecticut in 2011.

24 HOURS OF LeMONS

AUTOMOBILE ENDURANCE RACES ARE FUN TO WATCH. Endurance races for crummy, worth-less-than-$500 automobiles are more fun to watch. Endurance races for crummy, worth-less-than-$500 automobiles that are dressed up and unnecessarily customized are the best to watch. A punny spin-off of the more famous (and arguably classier) endurance race in LeMans, France, America's LeMons races—lemons are bad cars; get it?—are held at various tracks around the country throughout the year. The sponsoring outfit, LeMons, moves to different venues and hosts weekend-long events that test drivers' mechanical skills, ingenuity, and staying power. With tongues planted firmly in their cheeks, the LeMons powers-that-be have taken the world's oldest automobile race and applied their worth-less-than-$500 Midas touch, while tapping into the classic American rags-to-riches ethos. With decorated cars.

A parade of speeding misfits.

FUNNY CARS

The LeMons entries are hilarious. They are not, however, funny cars. Since the mid-1960s Funny Car Drag Racing has rounded out the drag racing spectrum. The origin of the name "funny car" is not as tantalizing as might be expected, but is based simply on the fact that once the rear wheels were moved forward to shift the weight distribution on the vehicle, the cars no longer looked like standard stock cars but, rather, "funny."

OUTHOUSE RACING

PROBABLY THE BEST EXAMPLE OF THE AMERICAN DRIVE TO MAKE EVERYTHING COMPETITIVE IS THE OUTHOUSE RACE. Because, really, what toilet is complete until you put wheels on it and hurtle it down public byways? Shockingly enough, there are *at least* four annual outhouse-centric events across America each year. The rules are essentially the same across venues: A pusher is stationed at each corner of the outhouse while the final team member sits atop the toilet. Decoration is the way to distinguish one's outhouse from the competition, but only the Virginia City, Nevada, World Championship Outhouse Race demands that the outhouse be actually functional (though proving it is not encouraged).

SELLING SEWAGE

What sewage company trucks lack in sexiness, they make up for with pun-tastic slogans.

• Caution: Stoolbus • Yesterday's Meals on Wheels • Money in the Tank •
• We Like to Potty • Thanks for Flushing Our Business Down the Drain •
• You Dump It . . . We Pump It • Your Number 2 Is Our Number 1 •
• Number 1 in the Number 2 Business • Dirty Deeds . . . Done Dirt Cheap! •
• Satisfaction Guaranteed, or 110% of Your Product Back! •

Even South Haven, Michigan, gets into the potty, punny spirit at the Fall Festival in 2013.

REDNECK BLANK, PIG ROAST AND MUSIC FESTIVAL

AT ONE TIME CALLED THE REDNECK OLYMPICS (there were some legal issues with using the "O" word, apparently), the Redneck Blank (get it?), Pig Roast and Music Festival occurs every year in Hebron, Maine. Based on the Redneck Games in Dublin, Georgia, which were founded as a way to provide sporting entertainment for those who couldn't afford to go to the Olympics, both annual gatherings feature a spate of events including the muddy tug-o-war, the greased watermelon haul, the belly flop, bobbing for pigs' feet, and wife carrying. In the state of Maine the Blank takes place on a rural farm and has grown every year since its kickoff in 2010, and the Redneck Games in Georgia have continued to balloon since their inception in 1996. A specifically American subculture, the gathering of "rednecks" listen to music, drink beer, and drive their various vehicles (giant tires on pickup trucks, golf carts, lawn mowers) through the mud—American pastimes that are loved by many, but rarely celebrated with such ceremony.

Joe "Nailbender" Pike dives into the fun, belly-first, at the 1998 Redneck Summer Games in East Dublin, Georgia.

HERE SHE IS....

SINCE P. T. BARNUM first tried to institute The Handsomest Ladies pageant in his Dime Museum in 1854, beauty pageants in America have snowballed in popularity, scope, and downright wackiness. Judging women on their physical attributes is by no means a uniquely American activity (Paris judged Aphrodite the fairest of them all in exchange for the promise of Helen of Troy's hand in marriage), but Americans' inherent competitiveness and commercial drive have given rise to more than a century's worth of top-notch, timely, marketable beauties.

MISS
AMERICA

HARVEST
QUEEN

MISS UNSAFE
BRAKES

MISS'D AMERICA

MISS KLINGON
EMPIRE

MISS AMERICA

ORIGINALLY DUBBED THE GOLDEN MERMAID, and part of the Fall Frolic organized by local businessmen, the Miss America Pageant officially began in 1921 in Atlantic City, New Jersey. The inaugural Mermaid was Margaret Gorman, a dead ringer for silver screen superstar Mary Pickford, who was rated most deserving by a combination of audience applause and a panel of artists serving as judges. She was young (fifteen), slight (five feet one inch and 108 pounds), and had the fresh-faced innocence that, on the heels of Victorian formality, appealed to Americans and their sense of wonder and expansionism. The rest of the twentieth century saw an explosion in pageants, and the Miss America Pageant is now an annual event that draws more than 25 million television viewers and features contestants from all fifty states.

What's better than a beauty queen in a bathing costume? A hundred beauty queens in bathing costumes!

Looking bored and beautiful, 1922.

HARVEST QUEEN

GILA RIVER INTERNMENT CAMP, ARIZONA. The Harvest Festival is an inspiring example of spirits undimmed. Nearly 130,000 Japanese Americans were held in internment camps in the Southwest from 1942 to 1945. World War II raged in Europe and Asia, and violent prejudice was pervasive. Executive Order 9066 demanded that Japanese Americans—American-born citizens, immigrants, and World War I veterans alike—were unceremoniously put in camps to, in theory, stem the (purported) tide of espionage and treason. An entire demographic was unjustly profiled and whisked away. The camps were ill-equipped and inhospitable. Participating in "normal" events was not just a coping mechanism. America had been in the throes of Beauty Queen fever for a few decades, and it reached as far as the Gila River Internment Camp in Arizona over the Thanksgiving weekend in 1942. Words are insufficient in expressing the injustice Japanese Americans bore in this dark chapter of American history—"sorry" isn't enough, but is purposefully written here nonetheless—however, these photos tell a larger, more profound message: The human spirit is optimistic, resilient, and indomitable.

A portrait of the Harvest Queen.

Above right and bottom: The beaming winners of the Thanksgiving Day beauty pageant.

MISS UNSAFE BRAKES

CHICAGO AUTO SHOW, 1939. Beer ads do it. Resort ads do it. Fashion magazines do it. And so did the Chicago Auto Show in 1939. A pretty girl is a surefire way to attract attention, and the brainiacs behind Miss Unsafe Brakes knew that darned well. In 1939 over 30,000 people were killed in car accidents, and the auto industry took some measures to raise awareness of vehicle safety. Enter: Miss Unsafe Brakes. With a form-fitting leotard and a head of blonde hair, she was there to bring in viewers to show the uses, benefits, and importance of exercising brake safety. Bear in mind this was before airbags (not a mandated vehicle feature until 1998!), or headrests (not prevalent until the late 1960s), or seatbelts (introduced in the late 1950s but not required until 1983). Cars weren't as fast, but boy were they risky. With her dangerous curves and suggestive skeleton that was both "revealing" and macabre, Miss Unsafe Brakes took the stage at the nation's largest auto show in 1939, showing that safety is sexy to the core.

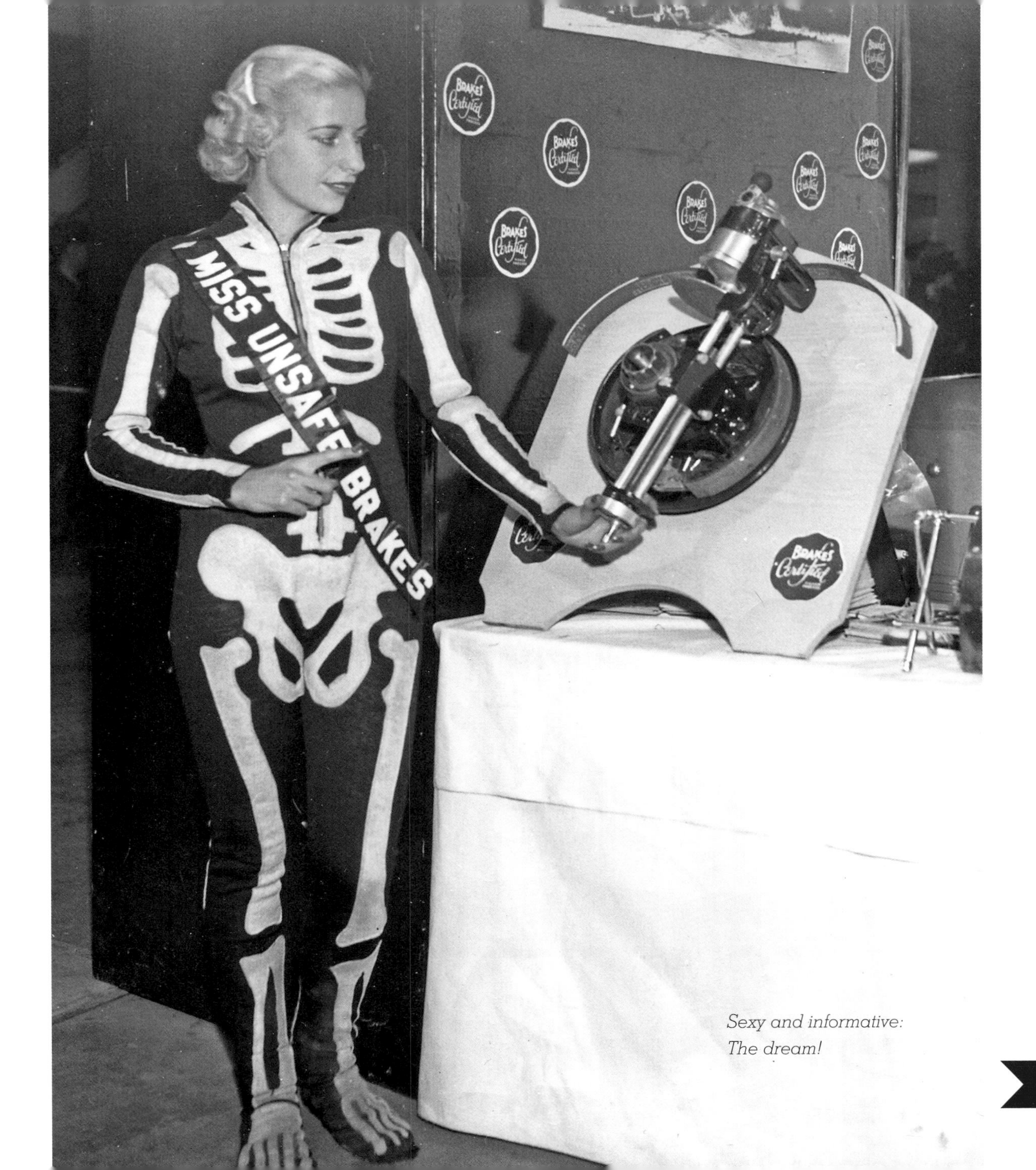

Sexy and informative:
The dream!

MISS'D AMERICA

BEAUTY KNOWS NO RACE, COLOR, OR CREED. The day after Miss America walks away, sobbing into her roses and clutching her tiara, the Miss'd America pageant gets underway. Started in the early 1990s, a beauty contest for some of the people who know beauty best—drag queens!—takes place in Atlantic City, New Jersey (the birthplace of beauty contests!). All contestants must be biologically male, not transitioning, and without implants, but are required to bring their best to the talent, evening wear, and swimsuit competitions. This pageant is not the only one of its kind, but has the distinction of being held alongside the same boardwalk that bathing beauties trod nearly a century ago. There have, of course—groan—been criticisms leveled against "traditional" beauty contests for promoting unfair standards of beauty and failing to objectively judge contestants, but Miss'd America and all her pageant allies encourage inclusion and acceptance and often provide much-needed (monetary) contributions for otherwise unsupported groups. There is no question that Miss'd America is, in a word, fabulous.

Big, bright, and colorful, drag queen beauty pageants are fun and fabulous.

MISS KLINGON EMPIRE

ta' neH, bI'IHba'mo' yImaq vuDIIj:
lovliness Salpu'DI' vaj 'oH not
juS vaj nothingness; 'ach reH pol
bower yImev 'ej Qong
quv yachtaHvIS, 'ej, 'ej yIjatlhQo' breathing naQ.
—*A Thing of Beauty,* by John Keats, translated into Klingon

ATLANTA, GEORGIA. For nearly twenty years, Treklanta (formerly TrekTrax) has been host to one of Earth's only intergalactic beauty pageants: Miss Klingon Empire. For anyone unfamiliar with the species, Klingons come from Qo'noS, their home world, and are a humanoid alien species with strict moral and warrior codes, making them fierce adversaries and loyal allies. The worlds and cultures in the *Star Trek* franchise are vast and varied, with Klingons being just one of hundreds of life forms encountered. The pageant, Miss Klingon Empire, demands that all contestants—human and Klingon alike—participate in the beauty, talent, and personality competitions to prove themselves to be the worthiest of Klingon queens. Trekkie culture is rich and enthused, and there's no question that holding the title of Miss Klingon Empire comes with many galaxies worth of pressure, and glory.

LOOK-ALIKE CENTRAL

Miss Klingon Empire is crowned based partly on how much she looks like one of the original characters in *Star Trek*. Not everyone can turn themselves into a dead ringer for the fictitious, so they may have to resort to a contest based around a historical figure. So will the real . . . Charlie Chaplin, Ernest Hemingway, Mark Twain, Marilyn Monroe, Elvis Presley, Vincent Van Gogh, Michael Jackson, Albert Einstein, . . . please stand up.

Though only one walks away victorious, the cabal of Klingon beauties will live to fight another day.

QUESTIONABLE FUN AND ESTEEMED TITLES

OR SHOULD IT BE THE OTHER WAY AROUND? QUESTIONABLE TITLES AND HIGHLY SOUGHT FUN? There is a fine line being trod with these festivals and their champions, but who are we to judge what is acceptable and what is not? After all, one man's trash is another man's treasure. So, too, one man's dream come true is another man's Mr. Mosquito Legs. Right?

MR. MOSQUITO LEGS

LITTLE MR. CHAOS AND MISS MISCELLANEOUS

THE HATFIELD McCOY MARATHON & THE TUG FORK TUG OF WAR

WORLD PILLOW FIGHT CHAMPIONSHIP

COFFIN RACE CHAMPIONSHIP

WORM GRUNTIN' CHAMPIONSHIP

DISC GOLF CHAMPIONSHIP

THE UNDIE 500

MR. MOSQUITO LEGS

THE GREAT TEXAS MOSQUITO FESTIVAL—CLUTE, TEXAS. The carrier of West Nile Virus, a headache for campers, and the unofficial state bird of Texas . . . Ladies and gentlemen: The Mosquito.

It's unclear why the blight of the outdoors would merit a festival since, in the height of summer, every morning and evening seem to become obnoxiously all about those danged mosquitoes. But every July in Clute, Texas, the lowly mosquito gets its day(s) in a weekend-long festival all its own. There is, of course, the standard festival fare: rides, food, entertainment. There is even a festival mascot: a twenty-six-foot-tall inflatable mosquito named Willie Man-Chew (get it?). But the festival also names a Mr. Mosquito Legs, a Mosquito Calling Champion, and a Miss and Mister Skeeter. Many festivals have their champions, so why should these titles catch us off guard? Well, the very idea of dedicating time and attention to something that most people endeavor to avoid is perhaps what trips us up. It takes all kinds, right? Yeah, all kinds of calamine lotion. Bam.

Willie Man-Chew sees all.

OTHERWISE UNSUNG OVERSIZE BUGS

Savannah College of Art and Design Bees

Enterprise State Community College Boll Weevils

University of Richmond Spiders

Alabama State Hornets

UC Santa Cruz's Sammy the Banana Slug

The Sugar Land Skeeters

Greensboro Grasshoppers

Fort Wayne Mad Ants

LITTLE MR. CHAOS AND MISS MISCELLANEOUS

WEIRD WEEK—OCEAN CITY, NEW JERSEY. A beach town is no stranger to the weird. But Ocean City, New Jersey (of course), dedicates a week in August to quirky contests. Each day in the weeklong celebration—the fest's second name is Wacky, Not Tacky—is a different contest. That's the Way the Cookie Crumbles challenges folks to chew a masterpiece out of a twelve-inch cookie. Saltwater, French Fry, and Paper-clip Sculpting challenge contestants to create the most stunning piece from the unconventional material. Ears Looking at You is for ear-wiggling enthusiasts, but the final day has the two events that feature the most no-holds-barred contests. Little Mister and Miss Chaos challenge three- to five-year-olds to make a ton of racket; they are given pots and pans and then let loose while the music of Dire Straits blares through the loudspeakers. The final, crowning contest: Miss and Mr. Miscellaneous. It's a talent show with the usual fare—singing, dancing, guitar-playing—but the contest has also attracted amateur acrobats, would-be comedians, and, once, a woman dressed as a cat who meowed. And meowed. And meowed.

No word on whether prizes are awarded to those who survive watching every potential Mr. Chaos.

THE HATFIELD McCOY MARATHON & THE TUG FORK TUG OF WAR

HATFIELD MCCOY REUNION FESTIVAL—MATEWAN, WEST VIRGINIA. The word *feud* immediately conjures two names: Hatfield and McCoy. The events leading to the family feud included (Civil) wartime violence, a fight over ownership of a hog, clandestine relationships, and a series of violent encounters that escalated until law enforcement, posses, and finally, the US Supreme Court got involved. Active fighting subsided after seven Hatfields were sentenced to life in prison, and an eighth man was executed. In 2003 the families officially came to peace, signing a document to end the strife. Though the treaty hadn't been signed yet, the Hatfield McCoy Reunion Festival was launched in 2000 and attracted thousands of people—descendants and strangers alike. The festival has food, fun, music, a marathon, and a pancake breakfast. But the tug of war across the Tug Fork of the Big Sandy River is worth the price of admission. The Hatfields gather on the West Virginia bank, and the McCoys on the Kentucky side. It's one of the most earnest and good-natured examples of burying the hatchet in America today.

This thar winner.

WORLD PILLOW FIGHT CHAMPIONSHIP

KENWOOD, CALIFORNIA. This is not your childhood slumber-party pillow fight. The contestants straddle a thirty-foot-long, greased steel pole and grab their weapons. Each is armed with a sopping wet feather pillow and must wield it using only one hand, but the other hand may not be used to grab the pole. Thwack! Thwack! Thump! One contestant goes flying into the large, custom-made mud pit below. The first to topple his opponent two out of three times is the winner. This semi-adult take on an otherwise innocuous pastime fits perfectly with the event's varied sponsors: the Kenwood Firemen's Association, Lagunitas Brewing Company, the Santa Rosa Rotary Club, and Hooters. The event began in 1964, but by 2006 had grown too big for its britches, attracting upward of 10,000 attendees. There was a widely pouted hiatus from 2007 to 2014, but the welcome return of the championships signals a new era for the feathered fights. The championships are now a traveling event, shifting between Kenwood and rotating host cities.

Top: When good pillows go bad.
Bottom: The inauspicious origins of hard-fought pillow fighting.

OTHERWISE INNOCUOUS WEAPONRY

Like the gentle pillow, there are objects that periodically get repurposed for less-than-innocent purposes. All of the following have been used for criminally nefarious, sometimes murderous, purposes and are spending the rest of their lives in an evidence locker:

Umbrella

Sweatpants

Pickle jar

Xbox 360 console

Prosthetic leg

Shoe

Spoon

Toilet tank cover

Stiletto heel

Crucifix

COFFIN RACE CHAMPIONSHIP

FROZEN DEAD GUY DAYS—NEDERLAND, COLORADO.
In 1989 Bredo Morstoel—a lifelong cryogenics enthusiast—died from a heart condition and was summarily packed in dry ice. He was shipped to a cryonics facility in Oakland, California, kept in liquid nitrogen for four years, then finally moved to Colorado, where he was housed in a shed behind his daughter and grandson's house. The grandson had been building a fire-, flood-, bomb-, and earthquake-proof house, and a homegrown cryonics lab in the shed, which is where Grandpa Bredo was stashed. Then the grandson's visa expired, so he left. The daughter took over dead guy duty, but was then evicted. A corpse-sitter was hired. With his descendants back in Norway, Grandpa Bredo was then left in the care of an environmental consultant. But worry not, because once a month, to this day, Bredo gets a visit from his custodian who, armed with 1,600 pounds of dry ice, checks on Bredo, refreezes him, and then seals him up tight. Every March, Nederland, Colorado, embraces the weirdness with a celebration of all things—well, *most* things—dead guy related. An Ice Queen and Grandpa Lookalike are crowned. There's a costumed polar plunge. A frozen salmon toss. And, the frozen dead guy coup de grâce, the coffin race.

Alive and well and on their way to victory!

COFFIN RACE BASICS

Teams of six pallbearers carry a coffin with a corpse inside through an obstacle course.

The corpse is really a seventh team member, and all racers must cross the finish line after making their way over hills and through snow.

The four fastest teams advance.

Then two.

'Til finally there is only one victorious coffin-racing team left.

WORM GRUNTIN' CHAMPIONSHIP

WORM GRUNTIN' FESTIVAL—SOPCHOPPY, FLORIDA.
Worm grunting is a real thing. Like, where do you think worms for fishing bait come from? Gruntin'. In Florida, where the soil is warm and moist and soft, the worms wriggle to the surface more easily, and more readily. Each grunter has his own rooping iron (like a large file) that he scrapes across his staub (wooden stake driven in the soil), and, as they will all tell you, it's not as easy as it seems. Getting the vibration just right takes time and practice, and that's assuming the weather and ground conditions aren't giving you troubles. The art of grunting is particular, and disappearing, so the annual Worm Gruntin' Festival in Sopchoppy, Florida, is a welcome opportunity to share knowledge and inspire enthusiasm. The gruntin' contest starts bright and early in the morning because the worms become more reticent as the ground heats up. The contest is for children, but the excitement is for all ages. Entrants have an hour to summon as many worms as possible, and then the champ is declared and given a $25 prize. Sopchoppy was once home to a whole mess of grunters, but today they are few and far between. The Gruntin' Fest may very well inspire a whole new generation of kids who want to grow up and spend their days outside with their hands in the soft, wet earth.

A beauty queen is only as good as her staub.

GET YOUR GRUNT ON!

1. Drive the staub (wooden stake) into the ground.
2. Scrape your rooping iron (large flat file or iron bar) across the top of the stake.
3. Gather your worms!

DISC GOLF CHAMPIONSHIP

MIKE THE HEADLESS CHICKEN FESTIVAL—FRUITA, COLORADO.

Mike was the unlucky fowl chosen to come to dinner one day in September 1945. Farmer Olsen axed the head off, but Mike kept on cluckin'. Sort of. A weensy bit of brain stem escaped the axe, as did the jugular, so Mike hopped off the chopping block and went about his business. Only headless. Not one to shirk an opportunity, Farmer Olsen grabbed his headless friend—Miracle Mike, now—and hooked up with sideshows to rake in a quarter per peek at his uniquely unique chicken. Olsen dutifully fed Mike's, um, food hole with an eyedropper. For eighteen months they made the rounds, but like so many viral stars, Mike's star flamed out when he choked to death in an Arizona motel room. Fruita, Colorado, Miracle Mike's hometown, celebrates his brief and singular stardom each June. There is a car show, plenty of chicken dishes, artisan craft and food booths, and . . . a disc golf tournament? One of these things is not like the other. Complementarity and relevance aside, the festival is a guaranteed good time with entertaining events, and attendees reveling in life and all its unexpected twists and turns.

Yield to Other Users.

Headless and proud, Mike the Chicken inspires disc golfers everywhere.

THE UNDIE 500

TESTY FEST—CLINTON, MONTANA.

Sigh There are no two ways about it: The Testy Fest's primary concern is *not* with keeping things "suitable for work." This is, indeed, one of the more unusual festivals in America, and the Undie 500 is quite funny. Even so, let's keep things brief.

The Testicle Festival in Clinton, Montana, is a serious destination for the fun and fancy-free. The ostensible inspiration for the fest is actually Rocky Mountain oysters, or deep-fried bull testicles—a decidedly regional delicacy. Well, from there it was a slippery slope to the wet T-shirt contest, big balls and ball eating contests, and the (actually) imaginative Undie 500. Contestants shed their outer layers (at least), and then race on tricycles. It's basic, it's funny, and it's kind of charming in a liquored-up-adults-in-a-field-outside-of-Missoula kind of way.

Training starts in the early years. Once an up-and-comer has reached 'maturity' it's a short, stumbly journey to a sloppy Undie victory.

THEY CELEBRATE WHAT?!

The Testy Fest is not the only festival that foregrounds something usually not celebrated.

EEYORE'S BIRTHDAY PARTY, AUSTIN, TEXAS

Christopher Robin can't go to this party until he's twenty-one. This fest is filled with bright costumes, drum circles, and more gallons of beer than Eeyore could ever want.

NORTHEASTERN PRIMITIVE RENDEZVOUS

For those who long for simpler, more dangerous, and uncomfortable times, the Primitive Rendezvous is a strictly period-accurate gathering for 1640 to 1840 Americans who happen to be living in the twenty-first century.

TARANTULA AWARENESS FESTIVAL, COARSEGOLD, CALIFORNIA

Not for the faint of heart, here's a celebration of the large, furry, creepy crawly that is the star of so many nightmares.

FESTS AND CONTESTS

CATCHALL.

Miscellany.

Potpourri.

You name it.

BUBBLE GUM BLOWING

KCYMAERXTHAERE SPELLING BEE

MOO-LA-PALOOZA

ROTTEN SNEAKER CONTEST

SUPER FARMER CONTEST

THE GREAT SALT LICK CONTEST

MILK CHUGGING CONTEST

MOM AND HUSBAND CALLING

LADIES' RUBBER CHICKEN THROWING CONTEST

DECORATED DIAPER CONTEST AND DIAPER DERBY

BUBBLE GUM BLOWING

HUMANS HAVE BEEN CHEWING VARIOUS FORMS OF GUM since the neolithic era, but in around 1870, chewing gum was officially patented in the United States. Nearly sixty years later, bubble gum was invented, Dubble Bubble being the inaugural confection. The inventor came up with bubble gum mostly by accident, and from the get-go it was regarded as a novelty. A proud papa, he loved to hold informal bubble blowing contests. Though Dubble Bubble held something of a monopoly on the bubble gum industry, bubble blowing contests quickly became a cheap, easy, and fun addition to fairs and promotional events. Dubble Bubble remains an active sponsor of contests, though Hubba Bubba has taken first place in aggressive publicity, being the official gum of the Cincinnati Reds and holding contests at markets during baseball season and then inviting champions to the stadium for the finals. The world record was set in 1996 with a twenty-six-inch (diameter) bubble, but that hasn't stopped Americans all over the country from warming up their jaws and throwing their bubbles into the proverbial ring; for the past century, Americans have been chewing, stretching, blowing, popping, re-chewing, and scraping gum out of their hair (use peanut butter!) in an effort to be bubble gum champs.

A strong jaw, plenty of spit, and patience all prove to be of no help to this beauty queen.

BUBBLE GUM FLAVOR

Bubble gum comes in hundreds of flavors now, including meatball, rose, sour booger, and frank and beans. But there are also hundreds of products that now come in bubble gum flavor:

- Bubble gum–flavored e-juice for vaping
- Bubblegum–flavored popcorn
- Bubble gum–flavored vodka
- Bubble gum–flavored antibiotics

And, no joke, in 2014 McDonald's was *this close* to including bubble gum–flavored broccoli in their Happy Meals. Seriously.

KCYMAERXTHAERE SPELLING BEE

THIS BEE IS FOR A SELF-SELECTING FEW. Held in Paris, Illinois, it is a traditional spelling bee in structure, but only includes words from a parallel world. Kcymaerxthaere (pronounced Ky-MAR-ex-theere) is a global project that explores the multiple dimensions between parallel worlds with certain nexus points on Earth where the worlds converge. And there is a mighty long list of mighty long words that are used to describe various ideas and principles. These are the meat of the spelling bee. And they can be as tough to spell as the name of the movement itself. The bee has been held annually since 2005, nestled within Paris's annual Honeybee Festival, and is hosted by the founder of the Kcymaerxthaere project, Earth's resident authority on the correct spelling of these out-of-this-world words.

Spelling is hard. Even for words that aren't from an alternate dimension.

WINNING WORDS

Here are some of the words that have cemented victory in the Scripps National Spelling Bee:

2016—gesellschaft
2014—scherenschnitte
2009—Laodicean
2005—appoggiatura
2001—succedaneum
1996—vivisepulture
1987—staphylococci
1981—sarcophagus
1971—shalloon
1967—chihuahua
1951—insouciant
1949—dulcimer
1940—therapy
1936—interning
1928—albumen
1925—gladiolus

MOO-LA-PALOOZA

COULD YOU FOOL A COW into thinking your *moo* was that of a fellow bovine? If the answer is yes (for whatever reason), then head to the Wisconsin State Fair to enter Moo-la-Palooza. Though *perhaps* not as flashy as its music fest namesake, Lollapalooza, Moo-la-Palooza brings out the best (moos) in its participants. The winner plods away with $1,000, a champion cow print jacket, and a golden cowbell presented by the previous year's top bovine impersonator. Oh, how we wish, wish, wish this were an audio book because you readers would be mooooooved (sorry) to tears from laughter at the sometimes impressive, but always memorable contest entries.

To achieve victory, one must have an intimate, close-up view of the real thing.

Mooed out.

CREAM OF THE CROP: COWS

TALLEST COW:
Daniel, Holstein,
Eureka, California;
6 feet, 4 inches

SHORTEST COW:
Manikyam, Vechur,
Kerala, India;
24 inches

OLDEST COW:
Big Bertha, Friesian,
Kenmare, Ireland;
48 years, 9 months
(1945–1993)

MOST MILK:
Gigi, Holstein,
Brooklyn, Wisconsin;
~75,000 pounds/
8,700 gallons (2016)

ROTTEN SNEAKER CONTEST

FOR MORE THAN FORTY YEARS, children between ages five and fifteen have been trying to earn the distinction of having the most repulsive sneakers in America, thereby having their shoes immortalized in the Hall of Fumes. In 1988 Odor-Eaters became the official corporate sponsor of the contest, catapulting competition into the smelly, stinky limelight. If a kid's pair of yucky shoes wins the regional heat, they then get to hoof it to New York City for the nationals, which are judged on three main criteria: (1) condition of the shoes, (2) backstory on said condition, and, of course, (3) odor. The shoddy shoes are judged by a Master Sniffer who has gone on record and said that the sneakers that tickle his gag reflex are the only surefire winners. The champion smelly-footed kid gets to walk away (barefoot, presumably) with $2,500 and a battery of well-earned official Odor-Eater products.

Montpelier, Vermont, is where, once a year, you can go to wrinkle your nose at the musky, ripe shoe-stink that only an adolescent can master.

CHUCK TAYLORS FOR A BETTER AMERICA

The Converse Rubber Shoe Company released the All Star sneaker in 1917. Charles "Chuck" Taylor joined a company-sponsored basketball team, the Converse All Stars, in 1921.

The godfather of athletic wear and punk style looking mighty pleased with himself.

Soon thereafter he began touring schools and local gyms to hold basketball clinics, and to sell sneakers. His verve for the shoe and the high-top's easy, flexible fit soon made the All Stars the most popular footwear for NBA players, Olympic athletes, and soldiers in training. By the 1960s, 90 percent of college and professional basketball players were wearing Chucks. Musicians and subcultures then integrated Chucks into their own costumes, as Chucks were becoming less and less popular among professional athletes. While they are no longer the preferred sneak for the athletic, they have become a hallmark of counterculture *and* wholesome youth. Chuck Taylors for me, Chuck Taylors for you—Chuck Taylors for a better America.

SUPER FARMER CONTEST

AT LOCAL AND STATE FAIRS ALL ACROSS THE MIDWEST, farmers and farm enthusiasts test their mettle in farm-centric competition for the title of Super Farmer. With a laundry list of events that test entrants' strength and skills, Super Farmer contests are an opportunity for hard-working, sure-footed Midwesterners to get recognition for the unique skill set that is required in agriculture. The official competitive lineup varies from fair to fair, but commonly found are the hay bale toss, wooden cow roundup, human wheelbarrow time trials, and fence post driving. Some of the more regionally specific events include corn shucking, potato digging, wife carrying, and egg gathering (which involves trying to find a hard-boiled egg by smashing eggs on a partner's head). And while the cash prizes appear to be consistently low, bragging rights are very real, highly prized, and a boon to any crop.

The county fair in Leesburg, Virginia, tests the mild-mannered alter egos of contestants, daring them to reveal themselves as Super Farmers.

SUPER FARMERS

James Cagney was passionate about soil conservation, raised Highland cattle *and* trotting Morgans, all while being America's Yankee Doodle Dandy.

Benjamin Franklin, when not being a Founding Father full-time, introduced Scotch kale, kohlrabi, Swiss barley, and Chinese rhubarb to American agriculture.

Johnny Cash, before his "Ring of Fire," was slinging bales in fields of hay.

Roseanne Barr's reality show, *Roseanne's Nuts*, was canceled after a short run, but America's sassy blue-collar mom claims that her organic macadamia nut farm is her most rewarding venture.

THE GREAT SALT LICK CONTEST

BAKER CITY, OREGON, gets an influx of weirdly shaped, oddly textured blocks of salt shipped to them once a year to be officially submitted in the annual Great Salt Lick Contest. A standard sight in pastures and barns, salt licks are fifty-pound blocks of salt with added minerals and vitamins that animals lick to get nutrients. Wilt Deschner, founder of the Great Salt Lick Contest, took note of how aesthetically pleasing (admittedly after a couple of beers) the salt licks the deer had worked on were and hauled them out of the mud, hosed them off, and set up an informal art show and auction as a way to, jokingly, put Baker City on the map. Since that first foray into farm-food art, the contest has grown and offers more than $1,000 in cash prizes for categories like Best Poem Submitted with a Block, Best Forgery (man-made salt licks), and, one year, Block with Closest Resemblance to Michael J. Fox. Since its inception the Great Salt Lick has brought in over $75,000 for research for Parkinsons, and continues to donate nearly all proceeds to help combat the disease. Some state fairs may have salt lick events, but Baker City, Oregon, has the distinction of being salt lick central.

Abstract. Postmodern. Cubist. Salty.

SALTY

"When it rains, it pours" is generally not a good thing; something crummy happens, and then a bunch of other crummy stuff happens. Originally, though, it was a selling point. The Morton Salt Company released the first version of its now iconic umbrella girl in 1914, along with a slogan that promoted the fact that their salt would not cake and clump up due to moisture. So, that's right. Every time you bemoan the onslaught of crumminess, you've got salt to thank for your choice words.

MILK CHUGGING CONTEST

SCIENCE SAYS DRINKING A GALLON OF MILK IN AN HOUR IS HUMANLY IMPOSSIBLE. Or, at the very least, ill-advised. YouTubers and trend hounds have confirmed this. Time and disgusting time again. There are officially sanctioned milk drinking contests, though, many of which are either sponsored by, or in support of, local dairy outfits. These contests are not intended to be dangerous, and so they generally only require entrants to drink a small container of milk as fast as they can. The North Carolina state senate has a yearly contest against the North Carolina state house where representatives form relay teams whose members have to down pints of milk in quick succession. It started as a publicity event in support of the North Carolina dairy industry and has become an anticipated early summer happening in Raleigh. Milk chugging contests held at state and local fairs are wholesome opportunities to raise awareness and support of dairy industries. The milk gallon challenge, though, just makes people vomit.

The Legislative Milk-Chugging contest demands that elected officials put their money . . . um . . . milk, where their mouth is.

VIRAL MILK

The milk gallon challenge has been making people barf since as early as the 1960s, but thanks to the geniuses at the MTV show *Jackass*, the challenge took the Internet by storm in the mid-2000s. The rationale for pushing oneself to the dairy brink remains somewhat cloudy, especially for the group of frat boys who took the challenge on a bridge and ended up "losing" both the challenge and their stomach contents off the bridge and into oncoming traffic, causing a series of accidents.

MOM AND HUSBAND CALLING

ANYONE WHO HAS EVER HEARD A CHILD CALLING TO ITS PARENT IN A CROWD KNOWS WHAT MOM CALLING IS. The Iowa State Fair has the unique distinction of turning those high-volume bleats into a competitive sport. Kids take the stage in hopes of calling to their mothers in the most creative and effective way possible, then walking away with the title of Top Mom Caller in Iowa.

ANYONE WHO HAS EVER HEARD A WIFE CALLING TO HER HUSBAND IN A CROWD KNOWS WHAT HUSBAND CALLING IS. Structured the same as the kids' event, Husband Calling puts more pressure on the comical component of the competitive call. One year's winning call was a woman singing her husband's name at the top of her lungs to the tune of Wagner's "Ride of the Valkyries." (Whether these calls actually work in the husbands' native habitats remains untested, however.)

Volume. Insistence. Threats. These seem to be common traits among the winners of Iowa State Fair's annual Husband Calling contest.

HISTORY OF HOLLERIN'

There is a long history of hollerin' in America, particularly in the Southeast, among both black and white communities. Whether it's to call the animals home from pasture, say hello to a neighbor, or alert others to an emergency, the holler is a distinct form of local communication. There are four main types of hollers, each of which serves a specific purpose and has a unique sound: distress, functional, communicative, and expressive. Hollerin' culture remains alive and well in Spivey's Corner, North Carolina, where the annual National Hollerin' Contest has been held since 1969.

LADIES' RUBBER CHICKEN THROWING CONTEST

SINCE 1994 THE IOWA STATE FAIR (the headquarters for more than a few wacky contests) has included the Ladies' Rubber Chicken Throwing Contest in its lineup of competitions. The name doesn't allow for much misinterpretation; it's exactly what it sounds like. The only rules are that the chicken must be held by the body, not by the legs or the neck, and that contestants use the chickens provided by the fair (it's no fair bringing in a loaded chicken!). There are two age groups—sixteen to fifty and fifty-one and over—and the three farthest throws are acknowledged. For more than twenty years women at the fair have stood on a hill in Iowa and hurled the mainstay of prop comedy as far as they possibly can, reaching distances of sixty-plus feet, while fairgoers watch the latex, plucked, flightless birds get their day in the sun.

Pick a little, peck a little. Pick a little, peck a little. Cheep! Cheep! Cheep! . . . Chuck the chick.

The 1981 bench for Stroud, Oklahoma's fun, competitive, and potentially lethal rolling pin toss.

IT'S BETTER THAN A ROLLING PIN

Before the rubber chickens were airborne, the Iowa State Fair featured a Rolling Pin Throwing Contest. The rules were the same as those for the fake chicks, but with heavy, long, solid-wood rolling pins. These would, of course, fly far and long, and were an undeniable hazard, so were given up in favor of the comedy staple. There was a male equivalent that could be found at fairs around America, called Wrench Throwing. This, too, has proven to be more than a little dangerous on more than a few occasions.

DECORATED DIAPER CONTEST AND DIAPER DERBY

MOST CREATIVE DECORATED DIAPER. State Fair Diaper. Group Theme Diaper. These are the three categories in the Iowa State Fair's Decorated Diaper Contest—a kind of competition that can be found from the East Coast to California. There is nothing unusual about parents dressing up their babies, but in diaper decorating, the cuteness is cut with competition. And though the elaborate and over-the-top diapers might not be exactly aerodynamic, winners of the accompanying event, the Diaper Derby, are just that. Sort of. The basic rules for that event are simple: All racers must be under twenty-four months old, accompanied by two coaches (parents, usually), and must cross the finish line on all fours unassisted. The distance is not long, but the event really does become a game of parental cheerleading—parents are at either end of the "track" doing everything they can to encourage and entice their babies to crawl their way to victory. Maybe only one baby goes home with a trophy to teethe on, but you can bet that every entrant is a winner in Mommy's eyes.

Competition is tough—and possibly teething—at the 2013 Berkeley, California, baby derby.

DERBY, OR NOT DERBY?

THAT IS THE QUESTION.

(Derby. That is the answer. Der-by.)

Though, 'tis nobler to investigate only one or two of these quests for outrageous fortune, methinks.

1. Any of several horse races held annually
2. A race or contest open to all, or to a specified category of contestants
3. A man's stiff felt hat with a dome-shaped crown and narrow brim
4. A boot or shoe having the eyelets stitched on top of the vamp
5. A hard-pressed cheese made from skimmed milk
6. A chocolate-dipped ice cream cone

DOLE AIR DERBY

ALL-AMERICAN SOAP BOX DERBY

FATHER'S DAY FISHING DERBY

ALL-AMERICAN DOG DERBY

THE KENTUCKY DERBY

ROLLER DERBY

DEMOLITION DERBIES AND DESTRUCTIVE MOTORSPORTS

DOLE AIR DERBY

THE YEAR 1927 WAS A HIGH-WATER MARK in aviation innovation, with Charles Lindbergh completing his transatlantic flight and inflaming Americans' lust for competitive derring-do. In August 1927, James Dole (of pineapple and canned fruit fame) put up a prize of $25,000 for a successful nonstop flight from California to Hawaii. Two army men, just the year before, had accomplished the 2,400-mile journey, and now aviators across America were looking to prove that they, too, had the right stuff. The derby seemed doomed from the start, however. Between the day that seeding was determined and the day the race began, four of the aircraft crashed and three aviators died. On the day the race was to start, some 100,000 spectators gathered in Oakland to watch the eight remaining planes and their fifteen crew members take off, despite the foggy weather. The first plane aborted over San Francisco with an overheated engine; the second crashed before takeoff; the third lifted off, then crashed a mile and a half later . . . You get the picture. Only two planes made it to Hawaii. Certainly, the Dole Air Derby and its high mortality rate is not indicative of the level of risk associated with most derbies, but it is demonstrative of the quest for fortune and fame.

A successful takeoff for the Pacific Flyer, *with poor* El Canto *lying mortally wounded in the background.*

One unlucky entrant who, after takeoff, didn't make it farther than this field.

ALSO HAPPENING

In 1927, when the Dole Air Derby fanned the fires of innovation and notoriety, here's what else was happening:

IN HOLLYWOOD: Films are eligible for Academy Awards for the first time, and *The Jazz Singer*, the first feature-length talkie, is released, changing the future of filmmaking.

CELEBRITIES: Clara "The 'It' Girl" Bow, Charles Lindbergh, Babe Ruth.

AROUND THE WORLD: Josef Stalin seizes control in the Soviet Union, ousting Leon Trotsky.

FADS!: Flappers and bathtub gin.

ALL-AMERICAN SOAP BOX DERBY

DERBY DOWNS, IN AKRON, OHIO, has been home to the annual All-American Soap Box Derby (AASBD) championships since 1935, with its 983-foot hill being the gold standard of derby tracks. With three age categories, three different types of cars, and multiple events for every division, the championship sends home a fair number of happy winners every year. Modern derby cars are assembled by contestants using official kits purchased from the AASBD. Historically, they've been made from orange crates, scrap wood, parts of roller skates and baby strollers, and, of course, soap boxes, but the frames are all made of fiberglass and officially sanctioned now. Gravity is the only force powering the cars, and there are weight limits for every division, so the main thing that separates the wheat from the chaff is the driver. Kids can train, and train, and train, and still only win by 0.001 second. Or lose by 0.001 second. The Soap Box Derby was formed in 1933 when a newspaper photographer got a kick out of local kids racing homemade cars in Dayton, and by 1935 it had found its home at Derby Downs and began the nearly century-long legacy of making kids into world champs.

WATERGATE ON WHEELS: DERBY SCANDAL, 1973

The 1973 All-American Soap Box Derby was riddled with scandal. Distrust was on the American brain, and Jimmy Gronen's mildly suspicious derby win was questioned by officials. He entered the derby at his uncle's insistence (his cousin was the champion the year before), and—again at his uncle's suggestion—built an electromagnet into the nose of his car. The magnet gave the car a tiny boost, significant enough to clinch the championship. Following the victory, derby officials took custody of Gronen's car, discovered the magnet, and held a widely publicized stripping of the vehicle, dramatically slicing the nose in half. Gronen was stripped of his title and denied the $7,500 scholarship that came with it. Gronen's uncle was prosecuted. A patsy though he was, little Jimmy Gronen became another example of the degradation of American ideals, prompting derby fans and the public alike to wonder, is nothing sacred?

Jimmy, looking happy with his trophy.

Speed demons.

FATHER'S DAY FISHING DERBY

DO YOU KNOW WHO LOVES TO FISH? DADS. DADS LOVE TO FISH. Do you know what dads want to do on Father's Day? Fish (with or without the family).

The Father's Day Fishing Derby in Lake Champlain, Vermont, has hosted a weekend of big fun, high-rolling fishing for dads (and non-dads) for more than thirty-five years. Fishing derbies are held all over America, year-round, but the Father's Day Derby is one of the longest running. These fishing enthusiasts speak a language all their own: "We were trolling with a dipsy diver while we loaded our dreamweaver ballyhoo cutbait colored with blue brine using a gold and chrome golden boy attractor." Uhhh, wut? The fish babble is unique to the fishing community, and these derbies are a chance to babble on with other babblers in a fun, fishy environment. And while fishing has a reputation for being a contemplative pastime that rewards the patient, the derbies bring a competitive spirit to the surface. Of course, that's more than understandable with upward of $150,000 in prizes to be caught.

The early fisherman gets the worm . . . on his hook, that is.

GREAT AMERICAN FISH STORIES

WHITEY, THE WHITE RIVER MONSTER, ARKANSAS: It's said to be the length of three cars, and to have peeling gray skin and a cow-like call. It overturned a Confederate munitions boat during the Civil War. It was aggressively hunted in 1937 and granted sanctuary in 1973 with the creation of the White River Monster Refuge.

THE FLATHEAD LAKE MONSTER, MONTANA: Said to be an American relative of the Loch Ness Monster, it is twenty to forty feet long with bluish-black skin and gray eyes. In 1889, when first sighted, it was fired upon by a steamboat passenger with a rifle. There have been sightings nearly every year since, with an alarming spike in 1993 when the monster was seen with a smaller monster (baby Flathead Monster?).

SEE IT?! SEE IT?!

ALL-AMERICAN DOG DERBY

THE UNION PACIFIC RAILROAD pushed through Idaho in 1906, and Ashton, Idaho, grew up as a railroad town. Come winter it was the end of the line, as plowing the tracks wasn't in the cards. Enter: the mushers. Dogsled teams provided the only way to transport vital supplies in the unforgiving winter months. March 1917 rang in the All-American Dog Derby, combining necessity, commerce, and fun. That race started with sixteen entrants, but the extreme snow kept twelve teams from making it to the start. The remaining four needed a second day to complete the fifty-five-mile journey. While they were geeing and hawing across the state, a small but enthusiastic crowd had assembled in Ashton for a day of ski jumping, ski racing, and a boys' dogsled race. The boys' race devolved into a literal dogfight with the boys trying to untangle their canines. The derby became an annual event and drew crowds of 10,000 to 15,000. With hiatuses during World War II and from 1963 to 1993, the Dog Derby now hosts multiple races, all named for the mushers who first trod them, ranging from 7.5 to 92 miles. There is a kind of festival atmosphere at the Dog Derby, but the focus remains on the races and the dogs that run them.

Yip, bark, woof, mush.

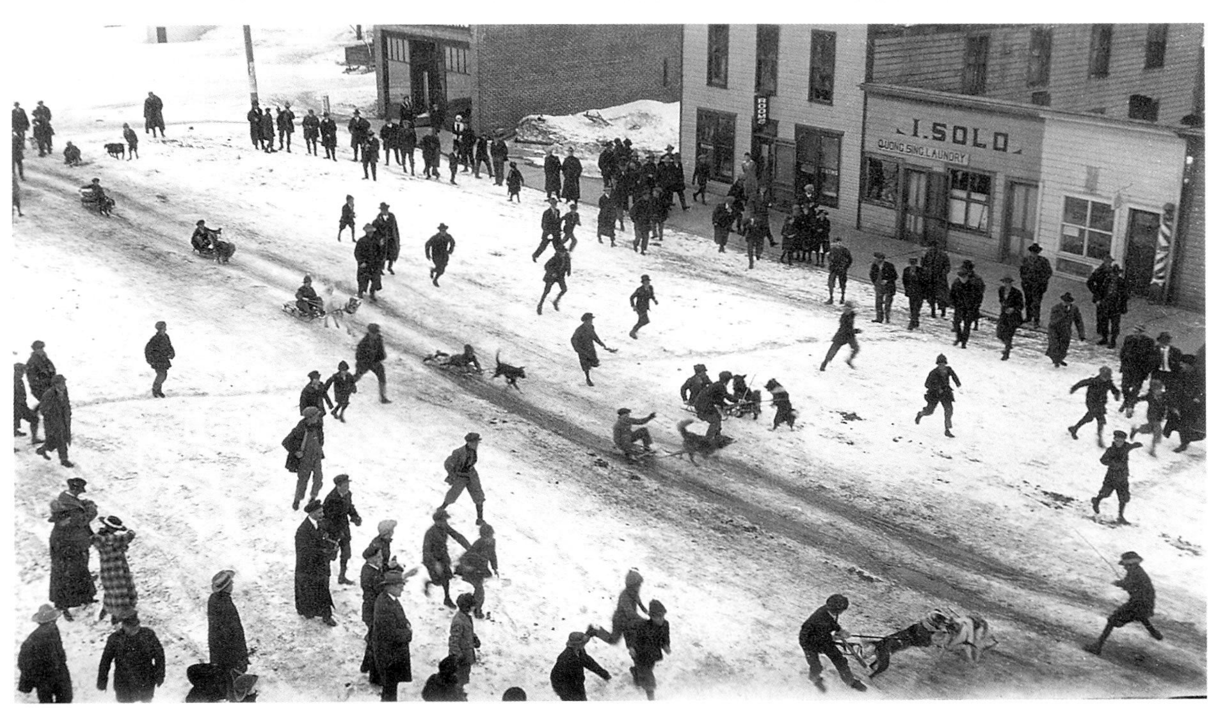

There's no telling who's mushing who in this photo.

THE KENTUCKY DERBY

THE RUN FOR THE ROSES.

The Most Exciting Two Minutes in Sports.

The most highly attended horse race in America, held every year since it was founded in 1875.

The race that was founded by Clark's (of Lewis &) grandson.

The reason Churchill Downs was built.

The first leg of the Triple Crown.

The race that now offers a nearly $1.5 million purse to the winner.

The race that put mint juleps on the map.

The race that draws the largest assembly of women in outlandish hats.

The race that Hunter S. Thompson called "Decadent and Depraved."

The race that merits a two-week-long festival before it's even run.

The race that attracts the rich and famous, including Her Majesty Queen Elizabeth II in 2007.

The race that generated almost $200 million in bets in 2016.

That's right, it's the big one—the Kentucky Derby.

These horses were born to be blurry.

Even while practicing, Secretariat commands.

EQUINE ROYALTY

The Kentucky Derby is the first leg of America's thoroughbred triptych. Parts two and three are the Preakness Stakes and the Belmont Stakes, respectively. Horses who win all three races are Triple Crown winners, representing the very best that American horse-racing has to offer. The list of equine kings (for they've all been colts or geldings) grew in 2015, rounding the number to an even dozen.

1919: Sir Barton

1930: Gallant Fox

1935: Omaha

1937: War Admiral

1941: Whirlaway

1943: Count Fleet

1946: Assault

1948: Citation

1973: Secretariat

1977: Seattle Slew

1978: Affirmed

2015: American Pharaoh

ROLLER DERBY

HEAD HUNTRESS. Sigourney Cleaver. YuNita Bakhoff. Rachel Tension.

Women across America are donning their skates, knee pads, helmets, and punny names to compete in bouts that draw huge crowds and intense loyalties. It started, like dance marathons, as a product of the endurance crazes of the 1920s and 1930s. In 1935 a promoter came up with the Transcontinental Roller Derby, which challenged teams of two to skate the distance equivalent to trips from New York to Salt Lake City, or San Diego to Chicago. One derby lasted forty-two days. The sport came to a tragic halt when, in 1937, a bus carrying many of the most famous and popular skaters crashed, killing nineteen of America's top skaters. As the nation moved away from the marathon craze, roller derby experienced a lull. Until, that is, it was televised in the late 1940s and enjoyed fluctuating popularity over the next twenty years while morphing from endurance to contact—what was essentially wrestling on wheels. With bouts being broadcast on a rotating set of channels, the sport persisted, but barely. It was around 2005 that the resurgence of derby-mania took hold. Today there are over a hundred teams in America. Derby culture inspires camaraderie and empowerment for those who participate. Derby girls shove, jump, fall, push, and skate their way to victory, and sisterhood.

A derby girl must be prepared to be the sprinter, or the hurdle.

DEMOLITION DERBIES AND DESTRUCTIVE MOTORSPORTS

THE VERY NATURE AND GOALS OF DEMOLITION DERBIES are destructive, dangerous, and chock-full of liability, so it's best that their production is left to those who've dedicated their lives to vehicular mayhem. There are motorsports production companies around the country, and each has its own niche: Stock Car Football, Kids Power Wheel, School Bus Demolition Derby. These companies are devoted to producing thrills and chills for drivers and audiences alike and are likely the ones organizing the derby hosted by your local fair. The origins of demolition derby reside somewhere in the need to dispense with prewar vehicles that became outmoded once vehicle production resumed in the late 1940s. Demo derbies spawned a subculture of die-hard fans and drivers, but these close-knit communities were small and regionally specific. In 1976, on the show *Happy Days*, the Fonz fell for demolition driver Pinky Tuscadero, and the derby was, once again, thrust into the limelight. Today, in an age that is increasingly liability-conscious, the destruction is managed by companies that offer not only entertaining mayhem, but insurance policies to cover it.

Amid the dust and the roar, demolition giants rule.

NO THANKS, I'M STUFFED!

In some cases, being the most successful at something is not necessarily a good thing. But good luck telling that to the select crew of competitive eaters found around the country. Rest assured that their levels of self-confidence are on par with their ginormous appetites: While most of us would gag (on an empty stomach) at the notion of downing an entire pie in one sitting—let alone *eight*—the following contests have bred a population of the iron-gutted. And, truly, giving credit where credit is due, the strong-stomached are among the few who can have their cake(s) and eat it, too.

GOLDFISH SWALLOWING

PIE EATING CONTESTS

NATHAN'S FAMOUS HOT DOG EATING CONTEST

THE MANHATTAN FAT MEN'S CLUB

ALFERD PACKER DAY SNACKER CONTEST

MOONPIE EATING CONTESTS

CUPCAKE CHOMPING CONTESTS

LA COSTEÑA FEEL THE HEAT JALAPEÑO EATING CONTEST

THE ILL-ADVISED, THE UNCONVENTIONAL, AND THE UNFORTUNATE

GOLDFISH SWALLOWING

THIS ENTRY IS DUBIOUS, AT BEST. For a host of reasons. First: Goldfish swallowing was a fad in the mid-twentieth century, and contemporaneous with other trends like phone booth stuffing and the ever-noble panty raid. Young people in America could not seem to reach a consensus on which direction their moral compasses were going to settle, so they took to things like downing as many *live* goldfish in one sitting as possible. And second: Apart from the not-exactly-honorable company it kept with its contemporary fads, goldfish were being eaten across college campuses. This seemed unduly cruel to the goldfish. And the swallowers! And the audience! Let us all thank our lucky stars that the trend was brief due to the quick—and often legal—acknowledgment that this probably wasn't the best use of young people's time. The short-lived and ill-conceived contests were put to bed on the heels of reports of one college student downing an astonishing eighty-nine fishies in one sitting. Who would even *want* to beat that record?!

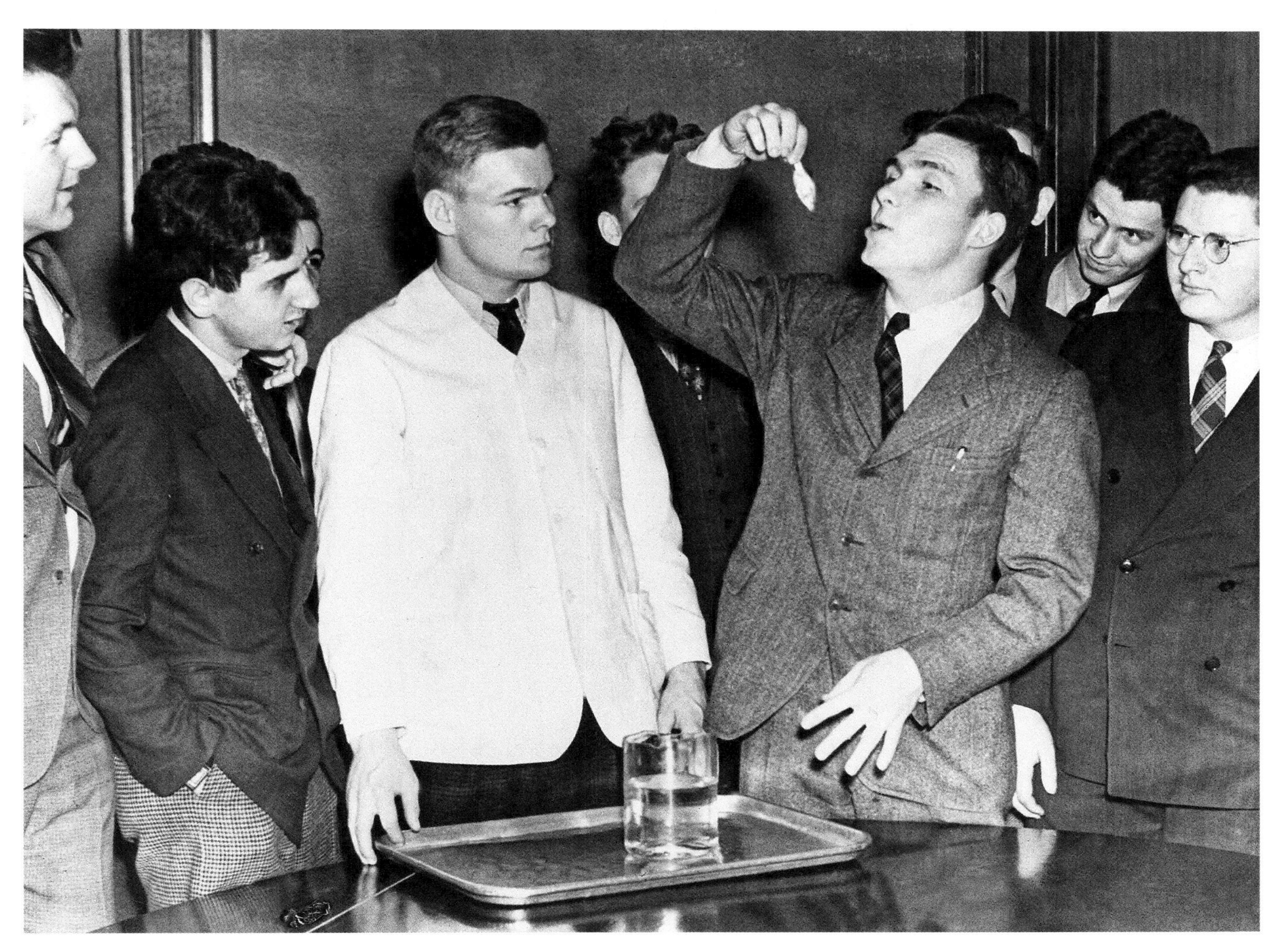

An ill-advised pastime at Harvard, 1939.

PIE EATING CONTESTS

FOR WHATEVER REASON, the scale and enthusiasm for cleaning as many plates as possible, as quickly as possible, is a distinctly American pastime. Pies have been the most popular and plentiful dish for quick and dirty public consumption for much of the twentieth century. A staple at county fairs for the first half of the 1900s, pie eating contests were also a nice way to feature specific agricultural products at specific times and regions: Blueberries, chocolate pudding, apple, mincemeat, and cranberries all have had their moment in the sun. While specific pie eating contests have not taken the spotlight in the way that contests involving hot dogs, oysters, and chicken have—except, of course, for the infamous and memorable revenge story-within-a-story in Stephen King's *Stand By Me*, after which a real-life contest is now based and held in Oregon where the reigning champ ate over nine pounds of blueberry pie in eight minutes (oy!)—their prevalence across time and regions has cemented (congealed?) their place in gluttonous history.

Vintage mmmmmmmmmm!

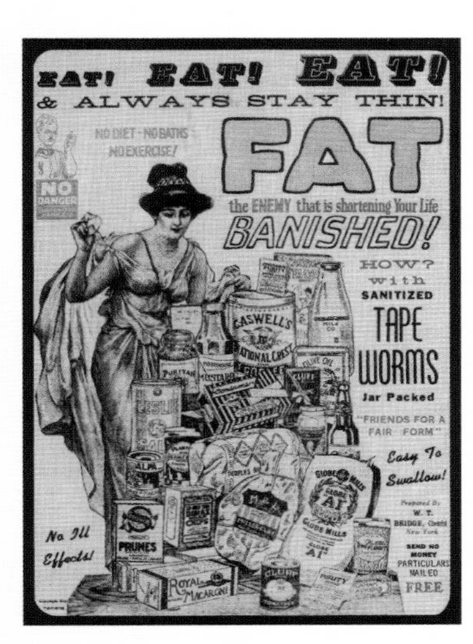

Eat! Eat! Eat! And Always Stay Thin!

THE TAPEWORM DIET

Swallow a parasite and eat to your worm's content!

STEP 1: Acquire magical tapeworm pills.

STEP 2: Swallow pills.

STEP 3: Watch your fat melt away!

Opera mega-diva Maria Callas was rumored to have lost sixty pounds because of a tapeworm. In 2005 a woman in Iowa went to the emergency room with stomach pains and came out with a diagnosis of "unwisely swallowed a parasite."

STEP 4: Figure out how to get rid of the tapeworm . . .

NATHAN'S FAMOUS HOT DOG EATING CONTEST

OF ALL THE EATING CONTESTS HELD AT HOME AND ABROAD, none is quite as famous as Nathan's Famous Hot Dog Eating Contest. An early entry in the overstuffed annals of competitive eating, Nathan's Famous grew and, indeed, germinated an Americana staple. The legend says that four men were eating hot dogs on July 4, 1916, at Nathan's flagship stand on Coney Island, and began arguing over who was the most patriotic. Well, they put their money where their mouths were and began shoveling in as many dogs as fast as they could to see who could truly stomach the most patriotism. One hundred years later the contest has grown to be one of, if not the largest and most prestigious of all the glutton-centric competitions in the world. The 2016 champs for Nathan's Famous (accept no substitutes) HDB (hot dogs plus buns) per ten minutes were Joey "Jaws" Chestnut with seventy HDB, and Miki Sudo with thirty-eight HDB, both well-established, surprisingly thin giants in the world of competitive eating.

Patrick "Deep Dish" Bertoletti puts his money where his mouth is.

Puns make everything taste better.

EVERY (HOT) DOG MUST HAVE HIS DAY—WIENER STRATEGIES

To be a winner you have to train like a winner! Here are some basic strategies from some of the world's champion eaters:

DRINK WATER. Then some more water. Then some more. Being able to drink a gallon of water in twenty to thirty seconds ensures the stomach will stretch quickly.

WORK THOSE MUSCLES. Don't spend all of your contest chewing, but don't slack off on chewing practice. Gum is helpful here, and some champs swear by the seven to ten pieces they work with at a time.

STAY IN SHAPE. The Fat Belt Theory maintains that if your abdomen is padded with excess fat, there will be less room for your stomach to expand.

CHIPMUNK IT. Getting as much food in your mouth at once is a good bet; once it's in your mouth, you can break it down before it even hits your throat.

DUNK IT. Buns can become a big, doughy burden. Dunking them in a liquid before they hit your tongue can take a lot of pressure off both your jaw and your stomach.

THE MANHATTAN FAT MEN'S CLUB

AFTER THE CIVIL WAR and before the Great Depression was the fat man's era in America. In decidedly medieval fashion, the more rotund members of society would gather in private clubs to socialize, and to eat, duh. Fat Men's Clubs were absolutely a celebration and encouragement of the more-than-full-figured: In fact, it was standard practice to have a strict weight requirement—"you must be *this* fat to be in our club" (usually 200 pounds). As the Roaring Twenties gave rise to the Crippling Thirties, so ended the golden age of the fat-cat robber baron. Not before, however, a particularly memorable meeting between three gastronomic giants. The three men, with a combined weight of just over a ton, met at the Manhattan Fat Men's Club in 1909 where they ate a combined weight of well over 30 pounds of food (26 of them being steak), including 675 oysters, 27 cups of coffee, and 10 pies. Though their club fell out of fashion not long after, one of the gourmands retained his status symbol as the alderman who, in 1911, very publicly had to have a chimney demolished around him because his bowl full of jelly had gotten stuck.

The Standard Magazine Section—Ogden, Utah, November 1, 1913

WHY FAT MEN ARE BETTER NATURED THAN THIN ONES.

They are Less Given to Worry, Therefore Experience Less Wear and Tear on the Nerves and When a Man's Nerves are at Peace, He Can Afford to Smile Oftener Than He Scowls.

As if we needed someone to spell it out for us . . .

TALK ABOUT FAT MEN! HERE'S THE FATTEST BABY, 5 YEARS OLD AND WEIGHS 214 LBS.

5 yrs. old
214 pounds
"Big Joe" Cody

BY LINTON K. STARR.

Mount Airy, Ga., June 27.—North America, attention! Terrestrial sphere, take note!

In point of ponderosities, the state of Georgia is STILL on your map!

Of all fatties EVER, "Big Joe" Cody takes the cake!

Georgia's on the job in the fat man game and jubilating, for we've got a

Little Big Joe Cody may not have been an official member of a Fat Men's Club, but his presence here should be unquestioned.

ALFERD PACKER DAY SNACKER CONTEST

BOULDER, COLORADO, IS LOVELY. Cannibalism in Colorado . . . not so much. In the harsh winter months of early 1874, Alferd Packer and six other travelers ventured into the snow. In mid-April, Packer emerged from the wilderness alone. A trial, incarceration, escape, second trial, parole, and ignominious death later, today Packer is (in)famous for his dealings in the woods (and the six corpses left in his wake) and remains Colorado's favorite cannibal. He is beloved for the tawdry details of his life, including his rumored conversion to vegetarianism. Students at the University of Colorado–Boulder took a shine to him in the 1960s, going so far as to eat their meals in their Alferd G. Packer Restaurant & Grill dining hall—"Have a Friend for Lunch!"—and periodically hosted a set of good-natured events in Packer's name. But it was only the first student-centric Packer Days that featured the Packer Snacker Contest. Throwing historical accuracy to the wind, students had to eat raw ground beef to win the Snacker Contest. This tradition did not last, and Packer fetes today focus more on beer and bacon but still retain that pseudo-celebratory, tongue-in-cheek (get it?) tone.

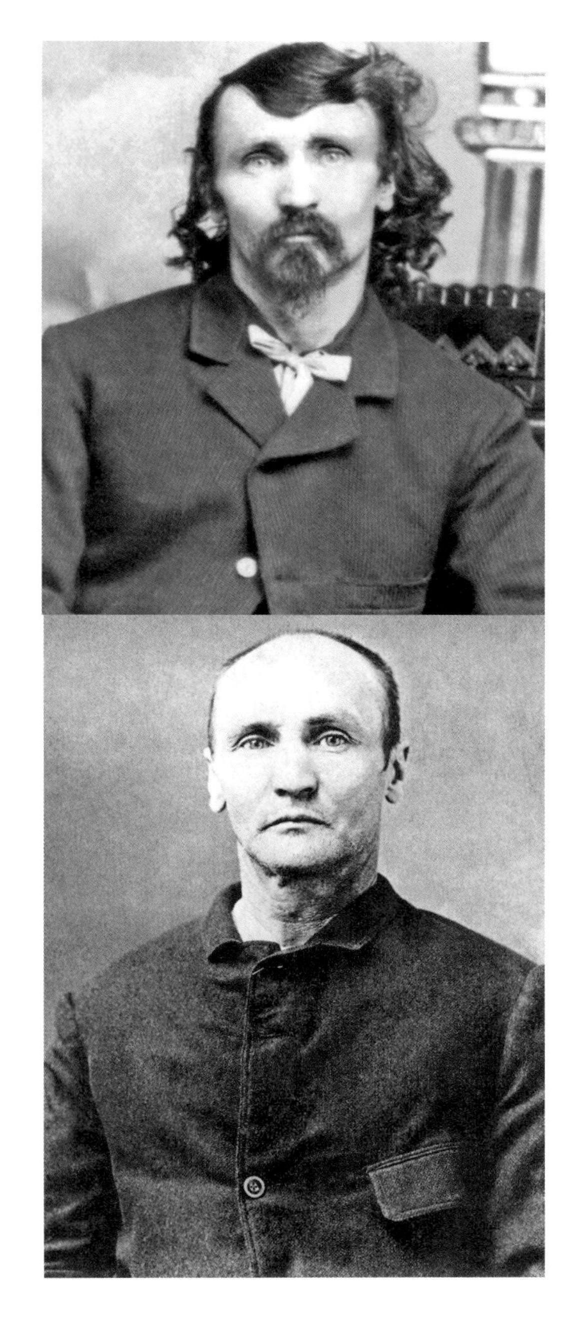

ALL CARNIVORES, GREAT AND SMALL

America's smallest carnivore: Least weasel—less than ten inches, deceptively cute

Smallest carnivore *ever*: (also) Least weasel—as small as five inches (including the tail!) weighing only one ounce

America's largest carnivore: Kodiak bear—over 1,500 pounds, nearly ten feet tall when standing on hind legs

Largest carnivore *ever*: Andrewsarchus—over thirteen feet long, weighing over a ton—the prehistoric dog/hyena/wild cat of your nightmares

Memorably voracious carnivores: A pair of male lions credited with 135 kills in Tsavo in 1898 during construction of a bridge by tons of tasty day-laborers

Packer before and after prison, where he purportedly converted to vegetarianism.

MOONPIE EATING CONTESTS

CHOCO PIE. SCOOTER PIE. WHOOPEE PIE. S'MORE. A variety of words, but an essentially similar treat. With graham crackers and chocolate and marshmallow come great responsibility to please, and the now century-old MoonPie has yet to disappoint. An absolute staple in the South, traditionally (and deliciously!) paired with its true mate, RC Cola, MoonPie is a year-round treat that, anecdotally, was so tasty that the first guy to ever eat one wanted it to be as big as the moon (hence . . .). These yummy treats have become a darling of the competitive eating world as well, given that they are a cute, manageable size, a little bit crunchy and chewy, and make for easy-peasy cleanup. Little kids and big adults snaffle them down in contests across the country. MoonPie Eating was adopted as an annual event for Major League Eating in 2015, with the world record—eighty-five pies in eight minutes!—set in 2016 when the competition was held inexplicably, and hilariously, at a BassPro Shop in Tennessee, the home state of the MoonPie. Chewy and lovely and utterly approachable, MoonPies, in whatever quantity, are an American standard that are out of this world. (Sorry.)

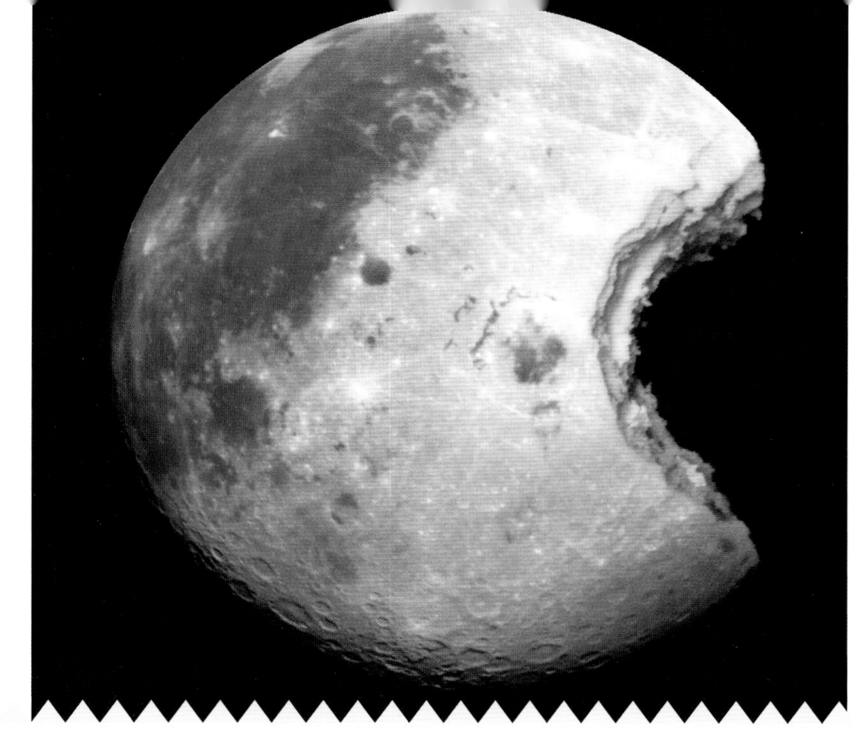

Moon pie. Literally.

FLETCHERIZE IT!

Health enthusiast Horace Fletcher was all about the body: how it worked, why it worked, and how to improve its function. After a lifelong interest in observing "digestive ash" (human excrement, yikes), he claimed to know the secrets to weight loss, improved fitness, and healthy living. "Nature will castigate those who don't masticate!" was his rallying cry. In 1906 Fletcher claimed that the key to corporeal fulfillment was mastication. You can eat anything, as long as you Fletcherize it; chew every bite at least thirty-two times (one for each tooth). Oh, and take a moment to examine your "ash." His popularity was short-lived and quickly outstripped by some other "out-there" claim having to do with the relationship between weight loss and counting calories.

Horace Fletcher and his powerful jaws, 1907.

CUPCAKE CHOMPING CONTESTS

CUPCAKES ARE LIKE THE MINI BACKPACKS of the culinary world; they're small, they're cute, they're trendy, and you kind of hate them if you see them too often. Not to be cowed by the risk of looking uncool, the world of competitive eating has loosened its belt and made some room for cupcakes on the roster. Many foods that are consumed on a competitive level come with a set of fairly standard rules—hot dogs come with buns, pies are eaten without hands—but cupcakes have proven themselves to be versatile, allowing for records to be set according to personal strengths. Sprinting: Four or six cupcakes are placed on the table and the gurgitator (contestant, eater) has to eat them as fast as possible. Short form: Gurgitators are given one minute to down as many cupcakes as they can. Big league: The more traditional six or eight minutes are given to see who can consume the most absurdly large number of tiny, trendy mini cakes. World champ Patrick "Deep Dish" Bertoletti ate seventy-two cupcakes in eight minutes, beating the former champ's record by one, measly, precious, cute-as-can-be cupcake.

THE LITTLE CUPCAKE THAT COULD

Mentions of the cupcake date back to 1796, with more recipes cropping up in the mid-1800s. They weren't called "cupcakes," but instead were known as "number cakes" made in "gem pans" (muffin tins). They were particularly easy and cute during the days of hearth ovens, as they baked faster and more evenly than high-maintenance full-size cakes. Cupcake popularity was cemented in the 1900s, but it was right around the year 2000 that the cupcake went viral and was confirmed as yet another trendy, super-cute, ultimately annoying food craze.

Diving into victory mouth first.

LA COSTEÑA FEEL THE HEAT JALAPEÑO EATING CONTEST

HOT AND SPICY FOODS DEMAND COMPETITION. Anyone who has eaten chicken wings with teenagers knows this: Spicy foods bring out the worst in people. Hot peppers—habaneros, chiles, cayennes, and jalapeños—when ingested whole, will be unfairly demanding on the human body at every given opportunity: The juice stings the skin, the seeds will start to burn on contact, the wicked juices make eyes water, and the flesh when mashed up will ignite everything it comes into contact with (lips, tongue, throat, and the, ahem, expelling parts). The stakes are high with super-hot peppers. So how the La Costeña pepper company has managed to find festivals and eating contests to sponsor for over fifty years is a question that gets to the heart of this book: In a nation that breeds one-upmanship, the most reckless dude is king. And, indeed, the ever-serious, always consuming Patrick "Deep Dish" Bertoletti proved he would stop at nothing when he "ate"—briefly, or corporeally hosted?—275 whole jalapeños in eight minutes. OMG.

While most people would give these peppers a wide berth, these guys supply them with a one-way ticket to their colon.

TURN IT UP

Scoville Scale of spiciness: 0—tame as old oatmeal; 2,200,000—the devil is hosting a barbecue in my mouth

0—Bell peppers: sweet, mild, universally edible

10,000—Jalapeño: moderate heat with skin and seeds causing burning upon contact

50,000—Tabasco pepper: sharp heat, source of eponymous sauce

350,000—Habanero chile: very challenging heat; orange and red varieties generally being the most potent

2,200,000—Carolina Reaper: top of the scale, world record holder, cross between ghost pepper and red habanero, sweet when bitten into, "molten lava" immediately following

THE ILL-ADVISED, THE UNCONVENTIONAL, AND THE UNFORTUNATE

SOME COMPETITIVE EATING RECORDS:

Kimchi—8.5 pounds, 6 minutes

Butter—seven ¼-pound sticks, 5 minutes

Mayonnaise—four 32-ounce bowls, 8 minutes

Salmon chowder—312 fluid ounces, 6 minutes

Rocky Mountain oysters—3 pounds 11.75 ounces, 10 minutes

Oysters (marine)—47 dozen, 8 minutes

Hard-boiled eggs—141 eggs, 8 minutes

Grits—21 pounds, 10 minutes

Raw onions—3 onions, 1 minute

Brain tacos—54 tacos, 8 minutes

Pigs feet and knuckles—2.89 pounds, 10 minutes

Turducken—7.75 pounds, 12 minutes

Peeps—200 peeps, 5 minutes

Fried asparagus—12 pounds 8.75 ounces, 10 minutes

Beef tongue—3 pounds 3 ounces, 12 minutes

Birthday cake—14.5 pounds, 8 minutes

Catfish—7.5 pounds, 10 minutes

Key lime pie—10.8 pounds, 8 minutes

7-Eleven Slurpee—22 ounces, 9 seconds

Cranberry sauce—13.23 pounds, 8 minutes

Fruitcake—4 pounds 14.25 ounces, 10 minutes

Twinkies—121 Twinkies, 6 minutes

Cow brains—57 brains (17.7 pounds), 15 minutes

Garlicky greens—7.5 pounds, 5 minutes

Pastrami—Twenty-five 7-ounce half sandwiches, 10 minutes

Chili—2¼ gallons, 6 minutes

Baked beans—8.4 pounds, 2 minutes 47 seconds

Cheesecake—11 pounds, 9 minutes

Cherrystone clams—26 dozen, 6 minutes

Corned beef hash—4 pounds, 1 minute 58 seconds

Ice cream—15 pints, 6 minutes

It looks like the onlookers are having a great time! Might not say the same for the contestants, though.

BECAUSE, WHY NOT?

LESS IS MORE, RIGHT? *Wrong*. More is more! And "more" is often achieved by acting on impulse and not saying no. If we *can* do something, we *should* do something. Right? If we *can* make kissing competitive, then we *should* make kissing competitive. If we *can* use a turkey for a bowling ball, then we *should* use a turkey for a bowling ball. Right? These contests and showcases demonstrate this oft-tested, rarely proven posit that "no idea is a bad idea." Though time and history have shown that there are, indeed, bad ideas, the competitive spirit is undimmed and the rallying cry reigns victorious still: More is more!

PHONE BOOTH STUFFING

FLAGPOLE SITTING

KISSING CONTESTS

ROCK, PAPER, SCISSORS!

UGLY LAMP CONTEST

UGLY DOG CONTEST

HORSE SOCCER

TURKEY BOWLING

MOST GIFTED WRAPPER

DUCT TAPE PROM DRESSES!

PHONE BOOTH STUFFING

IN THE 1950s, COLLEGE CAMPUSES WERE AWASH with frenzied group activities outside the standard sporting and social events. And without Netflix and iPhones, entertainment was all self-made. One fad that swept across campuses was phone booth stuffing, or crammin'. The idea was simple: get as many people as possible squeezed into a phone booth at once. Rumor has it that an ambitious group of twenty-five students set the world record in South Africa in 1959 and that many subsequent attempts stateside were all in an effort to break that record. But how could the record breaking attempt really count when "official crammin' rules" seemed to vary from school to school? Some required that everyone keep their shoes on, others that the booth be toppled and kids hop in it like a canoe, and some claimed the attempt didn't count unless someone could actually answer the phone once everyone was stuffed inside. Though no American colleges managed to break the record, and the novelty of the phone booth had worn off by 1960, the crammin' craze was reiterated in VW bugs, outhouses, and even hollow trees. No one ever said college students weren't pack animals. Seriously.

ALSO HAPPENING

In 1959, when phone booths were always occupied by one, two, ten, or twenty kids, here's what else was happening:

IN HOLLYWOOD: *Some Like It Hot* and *Ben Hur.*

CELEBRITIES: Frank Sinatra, Rod Serling, Huckleberry Hound.

AROUND THE WORLD: The Dalai Lama and a hundred thousand Tibetans flee to India.

FADS!: The oh-so-sophisticated panty raid.

Looks comfy, no?

FLAGPOLE SITTING

ONE OF THE STRANGER FADS TO PERSIST for the first half of the twentieth century was flagpole sitting. It was exactly what it sounds like. In 1924 Alvin "Shipwreck" Kelly was dared to climb a flagpole and perch on it. And perch he did. He stayed atop that pole for more than thirteen hours, and thus a fad was launched. Historically, column sitting was supposed to have been meditative and staid for the sitter, but this fad skewed more to the publicity stunt/unnecessary competition side, with copycats climbing their own poles soon after Kelly's initial ascent and setting records of up to three weeks. Throughout the 1920s Shipwreck Kelly would lend his perching prowess to various events, drawing impressive crowds every time. One stunt of his involved climbing the pole and then dunking doughnuts into a cup of coffee while doing a handstand (the man knew how to up the ante). Though Kelly's records were eventually broken, he remains the unofficial secular patron saint of sitting—still on top after all these years.

A clown on a flagpole. Seriously.

SHIPWRECK KELLY: THE LUCKIEST FOOL ON EARTH

Alvin "Shipwreck" Kelly was orphaned from the get-go, his alma mater was Hard Knocks, he did post-graduate work in hardscrabble jobs, and then he joined the US Navy. He knocked from job to job, including pilot, steelworker, and movie stand-in. In the mid-1920s he was at the height of his fame at the heights atop the flagpoles. He was said to subsist on coffee and cigarettes while perched, and would sit through heat waves, rainstorms, lightning, and extreme wind. Somewhat poetically, the fall of his career came in conjunction with the crash of the stock market, but Kelly never let go of the thought that his career might get reanimated. The 1930s were not kind to Kelly, and it's reported he was spotted most often in public acting as a gigolo. His final stunt was atop a pole in California where he had not one, but two heart attacks before the sponsoring organization was able to get him down. A week later he was hit by a car in the street in New York City and died there, clutching a scrapbook of his clippings that he had titled "The Luckiest Fool on Earth." Here's to Shipwreck.

KISSING CONTESTS

THOUGH THERE WAS AN OFFICIAL KISSING CONTEST held on Coney Island (a place that embraced excess) in the 1930s, locking lips for extended periods has made a resurgence in the past twenty years. In 1998 the Breath Savers company (three guesses what they make) sponsored a marathon kissing contest in New York City. To get to the finals, contestants had to make it through a regional semifinals, proving their lip-locking staying power. The main event was held at the Harley Davidson Cafe in full view of onlookers and passersby, where the couples with the most enduring love tried to prove to the world that they were the most physically committed mates around. There were no breaks, no sitting, and no breaking of lip-to-lip contact. The winners were flown to Paris, granted space in the *Guinness Book of World Records*, and awarded $10,000. (No word on whether they had to continue kissing once in Paris, though.) Since that contest—a publicity stunt, undeniably—others have been held around the globe, but the determination to be home to the most enduring kissers in the world remains a testament to America's romantic staying power.

Lip-locking in 1998.

IMPORTED ROMANCE

It seems a teensy bit silly to presume that no couples in America kissed each other and used their tongues before the term "French kissing" made its way to continental shores. That being said, the term is one most often credited to American and British soldiers who, upon returning from World War I, sought to embrace their sweethearts in the close, amorous fashion they had witnessed while in Europe, particularly France. The City of Love's influence came stateside and made a lasting impression on Americans, who remain entangled in an enthusiastic affair with close-contact courting.

ROCK, PAPER, SCISSORS!

WHY NOT MAKE A GAME traditionally used to break ties or determine who's "It," into a high-stakes, fully loaded competitive sport? Rock, Paper, Scissors (RPS) has gained traction as a tournament-style sport in recent years, especially since the formation of the USA Rock Paper Scissors League in 2006 and its corresponding annual championship in Las Vegas. The champ, if you can believe it, walks away with $50,000. The United States is not alone in its bizarre enthusiasm for throwing money and time behind this otherwise innocuous—one could even say boring—hand game: The UK holds an annual championship, and Japan (world leader in strange and possibly ill-advised sporting events) has hosted competitions with production levels unrivaled the world over. The origins of the game lie in Asia, and it was not truly popularized in America until around 1925. RPS roots already ran deep in the UK, and its World Rock Paper Scissors Club had upward of 10,000 members. The game has been used by everyone at one time or another to make some significant decisions (right?) and continues to be played the world over. The US delegates, however, have their tongues lodged in their cheeks as they take their digits to the world's playground to try their luck.

UP YOUR CHANCES OF WINNING A GAME OF CHANCE!

Rock, Paper, Scissors; SHOOT!

Rock, Paper, Scissors; SHOOT!

The first hand is, pardon the phrase, a crap shoot. There's no way of knowing what's going to be thrown by either side. Once that first hand is thrown, though, the game is no longer a game of chance, but one of psychology. If you win the first hand, you're more likely to place your confidence in the move that won: If you win with Rock, you're that much *more* likely to throw Rock again. If you lose that hand, you're less likely to choose the losing move again: If you lose with Rock, you're that much *less* likely to throw Rock again. As long as you can keep track of who's winning with which move, you can adjust your own moves to improve your chances of success.

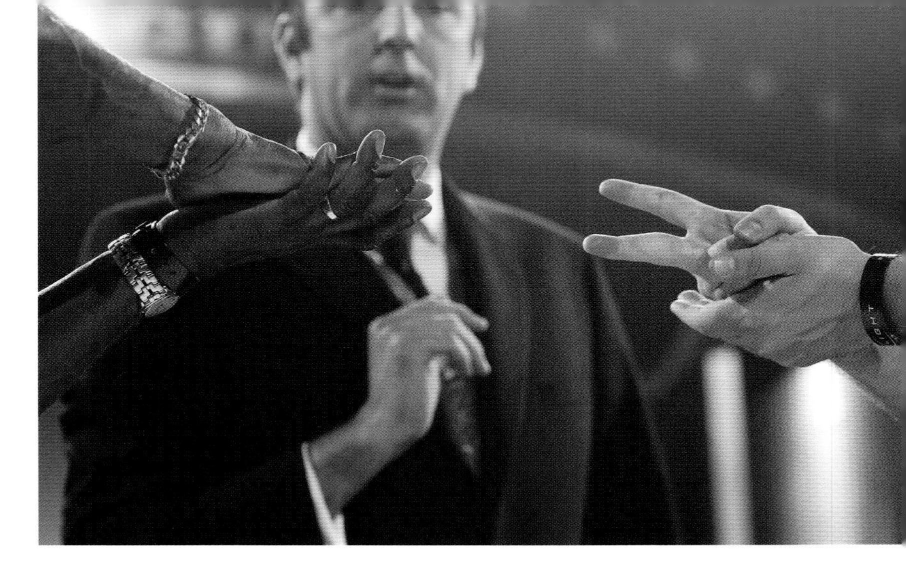

Tension runs high at the world championship, Las Vegas, 2007.

Even in its infant days, Vegas gleams like a beacon against the dark desert sky.

UGLY LAMP CONTEST

FOR NEARLY FIFTEEN YEARS the Kentucky State Fair in Louisville was "fortunate" enough to include an internationally famed Ugly Lamp Contest in its lineup. The contest was sponsored and hosted by Lynn's Paradise Café—a local landmark that had been featured on the Food Network and Oprah until it closed. In the contest's heyday, though, the Ugly Lamps came from as far away as Europe, and in all shapes and sizes, including a lawn mower, taxidermied squirrels, tin cans, and used gum wrappers. Americans' predilection for the extremely abject mixed with utility found a happy home in this well-lighted contest.

Kentucky State Fair, 1999. (Not pictured: a lot of really, really ugly lamps.)

In the wild the lamps are private and territorial. But come state fair time in Kentucky, they migrate and flock together, often appearing in clusters, where the true extent of their plumage can be appreciated.

UGLY DOG CONTEST

THE WORLD'S UGLIEST DOG CONTEST at the Sonoma-Marin County Fair in California features a lineup of contestants with faces only a mother could love. It is a testament to man's love for his best friend. The event, though specifically oriented to the deformed and the drooling, celebrates the diversity of the ugly pups, rather than simply lampooning them. The majority of entrants are pooches that have been rescued from puppy mills or shelters and are there because their owners can see past the bald patches and lolling tongues, to the canine hearts of gold. In addition to promoting the likability of the particularly pug-faced, the event has been a hotbed for pet adoptions and increased awareness of both the plight and the capacity for love found in shelter pups. The message is good and the presentation is slick, but make no mistake, the dogs are really, really ugly.

A face that only a mother—and an adjudication committee—could love.

HORSE SOCCER

SOCCER, which is "football" to almost everyone else in the world, is one of the only true international sports. Horseback riding is global, too. What remains a niche sport, however, is the activity that combines the two things. Originally put forth as a sort of training exercise to promote fun and skillful handling of the horse while encouraging the mount to be more social and at ease with foreign objects, horse soccer has caught on and spread like wildfire through the Midwestern states. The rules are akin to those in soccer (though without the consistently disruptive and slightly perplexing offsides rule), with the idea to have your mount "kick" the giant ball (between three and five feet across) to your teammates to score goals. While there are fewer overdramatized falls and scrapes, and rarely the confusion of a handball, horse soccer hits the salient points of being fun, accessible, quirky, and super cute.

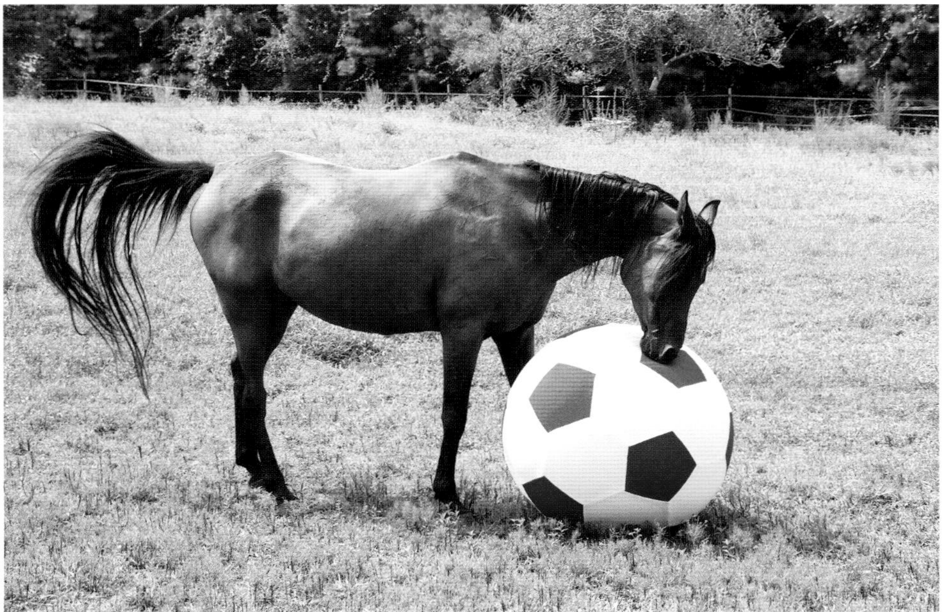

It takes time for horses to get used to the giant ball—these three are taking it slow.

Now we're showing that ball who's boss!

TURKEY BOWLING

IN 1988, AT THE NEWPORT BEACH Lucky's supermarket in Orange County, California, Derrick Johnson was going about his usual stock-boy duties putting things on the shelf. His buddies in the meat department, however, were sliding the frozen Butterballs across the linoleum floor. Johnson took one look at the birds winging down the gleaming tile floor, and a sport was born. The fowl line was established, as were butterballs (gutterballs), the wishbone (a 7-10 split), and the gobbler (three strikes in a row). Johnson threw himself into refining turkey bowling and promoting the sport, notably on CBS *Sunday Morning* and Arsenio Hall's late night talk show. It was his ticket to the big time, so he appointed himself the commissioner of the Poultry Bowling Association and hit the road without looking back. But the company behind Butterball turkeys took exception to the sport and its turkeys' place in it almost immediately. Johnson has since faded from the limelight, but turkey bowling has retained its place in the wacky American sports lexicon. Chucking frozen turkeys at a set of plastic bowling "pins" (often empty soda bottles) has become a Thanksgiving tradition at innumerable grocery stores, as well as at outdoor winter festivals.

Throwing frozen (wish)bones.

Pardoned and ready to fly the coop!

TURKEYS, AN AMERICAN/ INTERNATIONAL/ AMERICAN STAPLE

The forefeathers of our modern-day turkey were native to the Southwest and moved northward from 800 to 1100 BC, at which point they made themselves at home in the continental United States and began being used for their meat and feathers by Native American populations. When Columbus came around, he and his crews took a shine to the birds for their impressive appearance, as well as their easy-to-catch, tasty-to-eat character. Turkeys quickly made their way back to Europe where they became a culinary treat and status symbol. In the span of one hundred years, they morphed from New World wonders to European domesticates, so when the Puritans unloaded their stores and foodstuffs from the *Mayflower*, they were surprised to find that the turkeys they brought with them looked eerily similar to the ones gobbling in the woods.

MOST GIFTED WRAPPER

A BOOK. A CANDLE. A BOARD GAME. AN UGLY SWEATER. Those shoes you really wanted.

None of these would present a challenge at the Most Gifted Wrapper contest, held in New York City's Bryant Park until 2016. The nation's most proficient and creative gift-wrappers came to New York to show their stuff while competing for $10,000. The competition measured their speed, efficiency, and artistry in wrapping and presenting the objects at hand. Past "gifts" have included a model airplane with a seven-foot wingspan, a paddleboat, an oversize model car, a tuba, and Rollerblades. When live competition shifted to a sweepstakes format, people began submitting photos of their most beautiful and creative wrap jobs (and you can bet they weren't wrapping things like paddleboats). For those of us who resort to coating our gifts in a layer of the Sunday funnies with some masking tape haphazardly fastening the smudged edges together, winning this competition is as plausible as flying to the moon with our pajamas on. But for the hip wrap stars masquerading as normal citizens, this is their time to shine. (No word on whether these gifts are ever actually given, or how they are received.)

A finalist wends and wraps her way around a go-kart, and hopefully to victory!

PRESENTS PRESENCE

The first European settlers to come to America were not fans of Christmas presents, and, in fact, the practice was outlawed until the 1680s. Once officially a-okay in America, gift-giving boomed and ballooned. The Industrial Revolution saw a dramatic increase in purchased gifts, and the industry became so powerful so quickly that Macy's in New York City stayed open until midnight on Christmas Eve as early as 1867.

DUCT TAPE PROM DRESSES!

SINCE THE YEAR 2000, DUCK BRAND DUCT TAPE has been sponsoring the Stuck at Prom Scholarship Contest. No, it's not for prom-goers without a ride to the after-party, but rather for those who can see past the prescriptive uses of a material to transform it into something beautiful. Though the idea of donning an outfit made entirely from tape most often seen keeping ersatz bumpers attached to wheezy vehicles is not exactly appealing, a self-selecting set of high school students have found duct tape to be flexible and versatile, and appealing enough to wear to the big dance. There is no accounting for taste, style, or trends, but Stuck at Prom has elicited truly creative and stunningly executed formal wear from teenagers for more than fifteen years. With the promise of as much as $10,000 in scholarship money, plus Internet fame, the contest has attracted more than 8,000 entries since its inaugural year. As of 2015 that amounted to nearly 400,000 hours of work using over 90,000 rolls of duct tape in eighteen different colors.

2014 finalists in what was, undoubtedly, a sticky competition (!).

TWO UNWISE CLOTHING TRENDS!

CORSETS: Imagine wearing a top that is lined with bones, cinches in the back, and is meant to be worn so tightly that you can't move your torso, sit down, or breathe. Congratulations, you're wearing a corset! You, and the majority of women in the eighteenth and nineteenth centuries, can look forward to shortness of breath, dizziness, and eventually, the permanent and potentially fatal displacement of your internal organs!

DETACHABLE HIGH-COLLAR: Starched, white, and worn tightly against the throat, the stiff high-collar was a staple of nineteenth-century men's fashion. The collar was so very tight, though, that wearers ran the risk of being strangled if their throats swelled at all, or to asphyxiate if they accidentally fell asleep and their heads tipped forward. The collars were informally called *Vatermorders* ("father killers") but somehow that didn't detract from their popularity.

HARDER, BETTER, FASTER, STRONGER

SELF-IMPROVEMENT. CONSTRUCTIVE CRITICISM. Pushing the envelope. Shaping the future.

If something seems good, and positive, and attractive, why stop there? Whether it's cows, cabbages, or calisthenics, Americans continue to reach for the stars through encouragement, refinement, and an unstoppable drive to win.

VENUS DE MILO LOOKALIKE

LIVESTOCK SHOWCASE

AGRICULTURAL ROYALTY

AMERICA'S GIANT PRODUCE!

BINGO
(COW CHIP, OR CHICKEN)

WATERMELON PITTED AGAINST WATERMELON

THE MYSTIC KREWE OF BARKUS

VENUS DE MILO LOOKALIKE

INFORMALLY RUN FROM ABOUT 1900 TO 1923, the Venus de Milo Lookalike contest wouldn't have happened without the discovery of the famous Venus de Milo statue in 1880. It ushered in a new era of beauty standards. In conjunction with the new paragon of prettiness came a physical fitness and examination craze—the body, how it works, and how to perfect it. Thanks to the preoccupation with the physical, it was standard practice for college students to have their measurements taken upon arrival. More than sixty details would be recorded onto a card and then cataloged. One of the most prominent physical educators in the country, Dr. Dudley Allen Sargent of Harvard, collected these cards in hopes of finding the "modern-day Venus." Soon schools all over the Northeast were engaged in spirited arguments over who could lay claim to the most physically perfect female student. Things came to a head at the Physical Culture Show in 1922 when five women were poked and prodded (in the name of art? science?) before a "winner" was declared. But beauty standards had shifted dramatically by 1923. Venus was out, flappers were in. Though Sargent never declared any one woman the modern incarnation of his beloved Venus, it is safe to say that objectification was the real winner.

Left: Unrealistic beauty standards are not a modern invention.

Right: The Wellesley Thoracimeter.

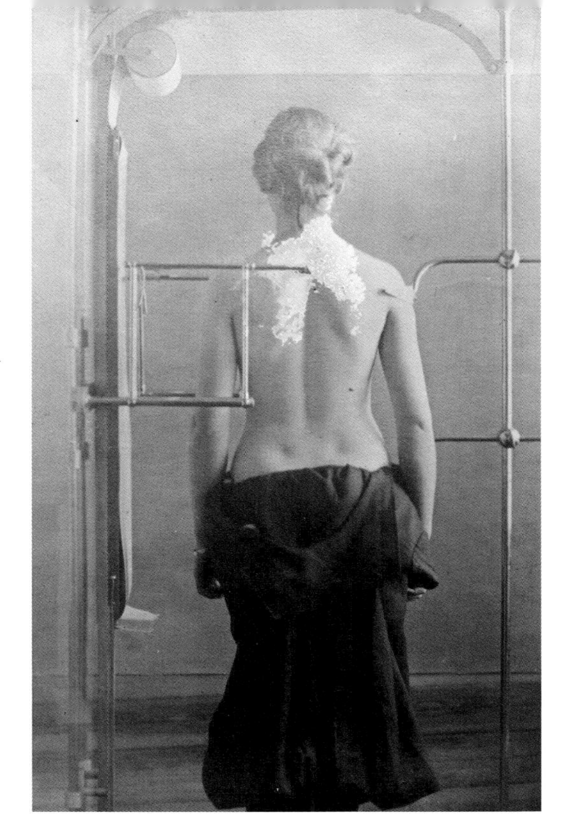

ALSO HAPPENING

In 1922, while young women were having their "traits" measured for their perfection, here's what else was happening:

IN HOLLYWOOD: *Nanook of the North*, the first feature-length docudrama, is released.

CELEBRITIES: Annie Oakley, Ty Cobb, Johnny Weissmuller.

AROUND THE WORLD: King Tut's tomb is discovered and opened.

FADS!: Stickball and speakeasies.

LIVESTOCK SHOWCASE

SINCE THE TURN OF THE TWENTIETH CENTURY, livestock showcases have become permanent annual events all over America. One of the longest running, the National Western Stock Show, has been running since 1906 and offers the largest exhibition of showcase animals. But agricultural and country fairs have long seen a tradition of local youths and adults alike leading their prized animals to town to talk up and show off. 4H—Head, Heart, Hands, and Health—was founded in 1902 with the intention of helping rural youth cultivate farming and agricultural skills. Showing off livestock was an immediate offshoot of that. Not long after, the FFA—Future Farmers of America—was incorporated, further growing the official participation in livestock showcases. And, of course, there is a long history of every cattleman, rancher, and sheepman's pride and exaggeration (in livestock form) having its heyday at the fair. Some notable categories:

- Champion Senior Beef Showmanship
- Supreme Ewe
- Grand Champion Market Hog
- Champion Broiler (chickens, seriously)

Pride and solemnity at the 4H fair in Stearns County, Minnesota.

Forth Worth, Texas, 1959.

AGRICULTURAL ROYALTY

SURE, WE'VE GOT COWS, but how about our cow queens? Or chicken kings? Some of America's most basic industries have been primped and preened to make them light and fluffy and easy to swallow. In the 1950s and 1960s, milk consumption dropped to an all-time low. Why? Because it was considered most vulnerable to nuclear contamination. Not that milk was actually ever tainted, but paranoia had the dairy industry hurting like never before. Enter: spin doctors. What better way to improve your public image than with a pretty girl? In 1948 the State of Wisconsin established Alice in Dairyland, which was really just a straight-up beauty pageant but nonetheless got people talking about milk. Fast forward to today, and Dairy Princesses are as numerous as US counties with dairy farms (a lot). Each year they are crowned based on their knowledge of, and ties to, the dairy industry and spend their reign promoting (and correcting misinformation about) that industry. But milk ain't alone in its use of pageantry. Minnesota crowns a Poultry Prince and Princess each year, and Colorado has its Cattlemen's Days Queen. (Alas, gone are the days of Nevada's Ms. Stock Grower.)

They truly had it all . . .

IF IT WEREN'T FOR THEM . . .

ELI WHITNEY AND HIS COTTON GIN: We wouldn't have processed cotton.

HIRAM AND JOHN PITTS AND THEIR THRESHER: Processed grains would be a rarity.

CHARLES HART AND CHARLES PARR AND THEIR TRACTOR: What would grace Midwest postcards?

HARVEY FIRESTONE AND HIS RUBBER TIRES: Tires used to be lined with steel . . . try changing one of those.

Without the inventions and innovations of a few super farmers, this is what modern agriculture could look like.

AMERICA'S GIANT PRODUCE!

A SHORT LIST OF AMERICAN RECORD HOLDERS IN GIANT PRODUCE:

PUMPKIN: **2,261.5 pounds (2016)**

SQUASH: **1,578 pounds (2014)**

WATERMELON: **350.5 pounds (2013)**

CABBAGE: **138.25 pounds (2012)**

JACKFRUIT: **76 pounds (2003)**

TOMATO: **8.41 pounds (2014)**

HOW TO GROW 'EM BIGGER

1. SEEDS: Get the best seeds possible for the kind of veggie you're looking to supersize; this will certainly involve some research, but if you're looking for bigger-is-better, then your seeds will likely come with the words Giant, Mammoth, Behemoth, Heavyweight, or Colossus.

2. SOIL: There's one word to bear in mind—*fertilizer*. And yes, that means manure.

3. WATER: Big beauties are picky about how much water they want, and when they want it. Many farmers use a drip irrigation system to take the guesswork out of things because oversize prize produce will not tolerate too much or too little, either too soon or too late.

4. REFINE: Be ruthless. Only the best will do. Thin your crop, then thin it again.

5. BE PATIENT: It's a virtue for a reason, and it will yield the greatest results.

The cabbage weigh-off winners, flanked by the faithful cabbage fairies in 2013.

The reindeer is for scale!

BINGO (COW CHIP, OR CHICKEN)

FIRST, YOU'LL NEED A COW. OR A CHICKEN . . .

So there's regular bingo, car bingo, celebrity bingo, and lots more. The two that take the cake for most unique, though, have got to be cow chip bingo and chicken bingo. A favorite fund-raiser event, cow chip bingo gets people outside and mingling. Chicken "chip" bingo, not so much. The bingo numbers are marked on the ground (or the bottom of the cage for the chikkies), grid and all, and then the cow, um, *marks* the squares as she sees fit. Invariably a lot of patience is required, as well as a readiness to compromise and negotiate about which square the "chip" actually fills the most. And chicken bingo is the exact same thing. But with a chicken. And usually in a bar.

This chick is ready to make a move.

BINGO BEGINNINGS

Bingo can be traced all the way back to Italy in the 1500s where a national lottery, La Lotto, was played with numbered cards and corresponding chits. The game spilled over into France and Germany, and was a European staple for hundreds of years. The story goes that a carnival hawker had seen the game played in Germany in the late 1920s and brought a version back with him to host at his booth at local fairs and carnivals. Enter: Ed Lowe, a prematurely tired and down-on-his-luck game salesman who happened to roll up to the local fair in Jacksonville, Georgia, only to find a crush of people transfixed by the game at the booth (like Bingo, but with beans as markers and called Beano). Lowe knew a good thing when he saw it and field-tested the game with his friends and family, one of whom was so excited when she won that she got tongue-tied and shouted, "BINGO!"

WATERMELON PITTED AGAINST WATERMELON

THE WORLD RECORD FOR WATERMELON SEED-SPITTING distance is 68 feet, 9⅛ inches, set in Luling, Texas, in 1989. The self-proclaimed "watermelon capital of the world" is in Cordele, Georgia. The largest watermelon in the world was grown in Sevierville, Tennessee in 2010, then again in 2013, by the same guy. The largest artificial (as in man-made and definitely inedible) watermelon is 25 feet long, lives on a flatbed, and is towed around Green River, Utah. The 2016 National Watermelon Queen is from Vienna, Georgia. With this slew of records, trying to compare them is kind of an apples and oranges scenario . . .

Picture-perfect seed spittin'.

Prepped to roll to victory in Brooklyn, 1964.

THE MYSTIC KREWE OF BARKUS

DID YOU MEAN: MYTHIC KRAMPUS OF BARTLETT'S?

(No, Google, we didn't.)

If there's one town in America that knows how to do parades, it's New Orleans, Louisiana. Home to the nation's biggest, baddest, and best Mardi Gras, New Orleans has a well-earned reputation as being a place that offers a little something for everyone. A "krewe" is a carnival-sponsoring organization, and the Krewe of Bacchus is among the most famous at Mardi Gras. But the Mystic Krewe of Barkus (get it?) is the only canine-centric parade of Mardi Gras, complete with a theme, and a king and queen. The event started as a kind of prank but quickly took hold in both popularity and good works (all proceeds go to help homeless animals). There's no topping their punning, so this author won't attempt it; previous Barkus themes have included: Wizard of Paws, Jurassic Bark, Tails from the Crypt, A Broadway Tail, and From the Doghouse to the Whitehouse.

A little pooch in his barkus box.

Smiling parade pit bull.

POTLUCK!

TOO MANY COOKS SPOIL THE SOUP

—No one at a food festival, ever

MOREL POLE

GREAT GARLIC COOK-OFF

FROG LEG FESTIVAL

BLUE RIBBON CRICKET EATING CONTEST

CABBAGE BOWLING, TOSS, DECORATING, BEER

WEST VIRGINIA ROADKILL COOK-OFF & AUTUMN HARVEST FESTIVAL

GREAT POTATO COOK-OFF

FLUFF COOKING CONTEST

MOREL POLE—NATIONAL MOREL MUSHROOM FESTIVAL

(INSERT JOKE ABOUT A "FUN GUY" HERE.)

Morel mushrooms are a delicacy, and notoriously tricky to find. Boyne City, Michigan, doesn't mind, though. Each year, on the weekend after Mother's Day, Boyne City turns into morel central, with morel-infused local cuisine, guided hunts, and the one-and-only morel pole. After the National Mushroom Hunt (you read that right), hunters can hang their quarry from the morel pole, where they'll be judged and awarded in categories like Largest Mushroom, Best-of-Show Mushroom, and Longest-Distance-Traveled-to-Pick-Your Mushroom. The festival boasts a morel tasting event that is alone worth the price of admission, and continues to draw thousands of fungus fun guys every year.

A GIANT delicacy.

FORAGE!

Morels are highly sought after because they are delicious and valuable. Here are some other edible things that can be got by scrounging:

ACORNS: Once cracked open it is important to run cold water over the nut meat multiple times to leech out the bitter tannins, then eat up.

WILD ASPARAGUS: Incredibly common and not too dissimilar from their domesticated brethren.

BLACK WALNUT: The green, dirty-tennis-ball shell belies the rich flavor of the nut within, which packs a nutritional wallop with a mix of fats, proteins, and nutrients.

DANDELIONS: Practically the entire plant is edible and extremely versatile. The greens are healthy and are often used in salads, teas, and even wine making.

TRUFFLES: Trickiest, rarest, and most valuable of forage finds, though good luck competing with goal-oriented truffle pigs.

GREAT GARLIC COOK-OFF—GILROY GARLIC FESTIVAL

SINCE 1978 GILROY, CALIFORNIA, has been home to the largest garlic festival in the country. The local economy relies heavily on the "stinking rose"—a charming sobriquet—and the annual fest celebrates the community's tight ties to garlic. In the nearly forty years it's been around, the festival has raised more than $11 million for local charities and nonprofits. The festival has grown to be one of the largest food festivals in the country and offers the tempting prize of $5,000 to the person with the best original garlic recipe. The Great Garlic Cook-Off happens every year and has seen such awesome, breath-wrecking dishes as Garlic Country Cornmeal Scones, Garlic Marnier Duck Potstickers, and Spicy Garlic Butter Cookies with Garlic Goat Cheese and Honey. Wow. Of course, in addition to the hard-fought cook-off, you'll find all things garlic at the fest, including free garlic ice cream, a host of other cooking competitions, a pageant to crown that year's Miss Garlic Festival Queen, and a chance to meet Herbie, the (merely semi-terrifying) Garlic Fest mascot.

Garlic, anthropomorphized and enlarged.

Herbie, the head of garlic, gets some love from some pint-size fans.

OVERSIZED AND STRANGE

If Herbie is the strangest mascot you've seen, then buckle up:

Steely McBeam, Pittsburgh Steelers

Zippy the Kangaroo, Akron Zips

Stanford Tree, Stanford University

And, you remember Willie Man Chew, right?

Yikes.

FROG LEG FESTIVAL

OKAY, OKAY. There *might* not be a particularly unusual contest at this festival, but with a focus like frog legs, the bar for uniqueness is already set pretty high. Given that the festival is positively saturated in frog leg propaganda, just attending is entering a contest: Fellsmere dares you *not* to try the amphibious snack. Every January, Fellsmere, Florida (where else?), opens its doors to any and all who are tempted by the words "frog legs" and "gator tails" and "dinner." In the days leading up to the fest, they stockpile the bounty of local frog giggers (think: spear with tiny trident) to prepare for the world's largest frog leg festival, where they will serve more than 7,000 pounds of frog legs (how many frogs is that?). Said to taste like a mix of chicken and fish, with a texture akin to chicken wings, frog legs are not exactly common fare, even in the South, but have made inroads into popular cuisine so that people don't necessarily jump back at the thought of eating them.

Where the magic happens . . .

The "before" photo.

BLUE RIBBON CRICKET EATING CONTEST

ENTOMOPHAGY. ENTOMOPHAGY. ENTOMOPHAGY.

Now ten times fast!

Super effective as a tongue-twister, questionably attractive as an appetite-whetter. The definition of entomophagy is "the practice of eating insects, especially by people." See where this is going? For some years now the Denver County Fair in Colorado has featured a Blue Ribbon Cricket Eating Contest alongside the more traditional fair fare. This contest is both kooky and indicative of the growing interest in insects-as-food. As the public has become more aware of the benefits of bugs-as-food, and since bugs-as-food is poised to become the next culinary trend, contests like Denver County's may well infest local fairs all over America. Though the contest relies on a brave and daring crowd to pull contestants from, it should come as no surprise that kids are the most adventurous diners, even when offered crickets well done or mealworms straight from the skillet. But with an increased acceptance of things like cricket flour (just what it sounds like), grown-ups might be unwitting adventurers relatively soon.

Edible? Check. Appetizing? Eh . . .

BUG MYTHS, DE-BUGGED

Q: Does a human consume an average of seven spiders per year in his or her sleep?

A: NO. The spider is more scared of you than you are of it. It wants nothing to do with your snoring mouth.

Q: Are daddy longlegs super venomous, just with fangs too weak to pierce skin?

A: OPPOSITE. They have fangs, but no venom, and aren't even spiders.

Q: Aren't bedbugs only attracted to places, or people, that are unclean?

A: YEAH RIGHT. Bedbugs are equal opportunity creeps.

Q: Won't cockroaches outlive us all? Right through nuclear fallout?

A: NOPE. Cockroaches are surprisingly sensitive.

Q: Is it true that a chocolate bar contains an average of eight insect parts?

A: OMG. Eight is not correct, the number is way higher.

CABBAGE BOWLING, TOSS, DECORATING, BEER–SAUERKRAUT WEEKEND

AN UGLY STEPSISTER VEGGIE finally gets its day. Phelps, New York, has a unique and specific appreciation for the cabbage, for without it, sauerkraut would not be possible. And without sauerkraut, the now fifty-years-running Sauerkraut Weekend wouldn't make such sense. In August the historic, picturesque town relinquishes itself to all things sauerkraut to acknowledge the town's long history with the historic, not-exactly-picturesque foodstuff. Phelps was home to the country's largest sauerkraut producer for a good part of the twentieth century. The company has moved and the cabbage is found elsewhere now, but the strong (briny, fermented) memory remains. The festival is still expanding. Most recently a cabbage catapult toss was added, because, why not? There is also an annual cabbage decorating contest for kiddies, sauerkraut beer for the oldies, and cabbage bowling for lovers of charming wackiness of all ages.

It's hard to say if a pin is worth more if the "ball" is destroyed when knocking it over.

SAUERKRAUT SAVED THE WORLD

Well, sort of. When the British ruled the seas—the Age of Sail, circa 1500 to 1860s—dangers and enemies were everywhere, but none was so persistent, or ruthless, as scurvy. Resulting from a severe vitamin C deficiency, an estimated 2 million sailors fell victim to the horrible disease. But in 1768 Captain James Cook sailed from England with 7,860 pounds of sauerkraut on board. His journey would last for over three years and took him from Tahiti, to Tierra del Fuego, to New Zealand, to South Africa. Though he and the crew certainly feasted on local offerings when they were warmly welcomed (not a guarantee, by any means), the briny, fermented tons of sauerkraut were almost certainly what kept them from succumbing to scurvy. Upon returning to England, scurvy had not claimed a single victim. Captain Cook was an integral player in mapping the seas, and world history surely would have suffered had he died of scurvy. But he didn't. All thanks to sauerkraut. (Mostly.)

WEST VIRGINIA ROADKILL COOK-OFF & AUTUMN HARVEST FESTIVAL

(YES, IT'S EXACTLY WHAT IT SOUNDS LIKE.)

The 2016 prize winners:

FIRST PLACE:

One Ton Won Tons: Smashed Pota"doe" Patties

Chinese Chef Boar R-D Noodles

T-Boned Elk over Grits

Thumper Bumper over Grits (Roadkill featured: venison, boar, rabbit, and elk)

SECOND PLACE:

Rest in Bits and Pieces—6 Feet Under Greener Pastures
(Roadkill featured: venison, duck, chukar [partridge], pheasant, and quail)

THIRD PLACE:

I Wanna Iguana Nachos (Roadkill featured: iguana)

RULES OF THE ROADKILL

ARIZONA: Animals may only be taken after procuring a big game salvage permit from a peace officer.

ALASKA: Moose and caribou roadkill are considered state property—a state trooper or the Department of Fish and Game must be contacted at which point they will have the carcass dressed (assuming it's "not too smooshed") and given to charity.

KENTUCKY: Taxidermy requires a license, but the creation of garments from inedible parts does not.

OREGON: Big game roadkill may not be collected by anyone; nonprotected animals may be collected by everyone.

WISCONSIN: A motorist can claim a carcass if he obtains a tag from authorities; if he doesn't want it, then anyone may request a tag for said carcass.

Bon appétit.

Always look both ways before crossing the street.

Rules for camel roadkill are unclear . . .

GREAT POTATO COOK-OFF—BARNESVILLE POTATO DAYS

CALLING ALL SPEC-TATERS AND SPUDDING CHEFS!

Barnesville, Minnesota, takes its love of potatoes seriously. The starchy staple celebration has been steadily growing over the years. Potato Days covers forty-eight hours of tater-centric events, including the standard potato sack races and mass french fry feeding ground, but also mashed potato wrestling, potato peeling contests, and the Great Potato Cook-Off. The rules are as basic and straightforward as potatoes themselves: Make a dish that uses white potatoes. That's it. What the lack of restriction allows for is a proliferation of creativity. In fact, the theme of the 2016 cook-off was "Anything Goes." Past winners have included recipes like Potato-Clam Soup, Savory Potato Chiffon, and Crabby Potatoes. One event that does *not* allow for much deviation is the National Lefse Cook-Off, as cooks from near and far try to outdo each other in making the tastiest and prettiest lefse (a Norwegian potato pastry resembling a tortilla). Both these cooking events are highly anticipated and hard fought. No room for weenie potatoes here.

Before the sport matured into mashed tater wrestlin', spud sacks were the means to a competitive end.

THE POTATO'S JOURNEY

The Incas in Peru cultivated potatoes, and Spanish conquistadors brought them to Europe in the early 1500s. The first potatoes landed in colonial America when the governor of Bermuda sent them as a gift to the governor of Virginia in 1621. And though now ubiquitous in the United States, the first permanent crop didn't come about until around 1720 in New Hampshire.

FLUFF COOKING CONTEST—WHAT THE FLUFF? FESTIVAL

ONE WOULD BE HARD-PRESSED TO CALL MARSHMALLOW FLUFF anything other than uniquely American. Rice Krispie treats and Fluffernutters are not what anyone would call international cuisine. In celebration of this American-as-apple-pie foodstuff, Somerville, Massachusetts, holds an annual one-day What the Fluff? Festival jam-packed with sticky, sweet events. Unquestionably jocund and messy, the fest serves as a tribute to the invention of Fluff by Archibald Query in Union Square, Massachusetts, in 1917 (though the fest hasn't been around that long). The cooking contest is standard in its structure, but attracts some mighty creative entries, all of which utilize the sugary marshmallow spread. Some winners from years past have included Cluster Fluffs, Peanut Butter & Banana Fluffsicles, Honey Thyme Treats, and, of course, Pumpkin and Sriracha Fluffenadas with Tomato Fluff Chutney. Past fests have included Flufferettes (Fluff-bedecked showgirls), Fluff jousting (don't get whacked with the Fluff-smeared foam noodle), and Fluff hairdos (styles created using Fluff instead of mousse).

A Fluff official with bags of Fluff in its most primitive form: marshmallows.

Fluff stylists are hard to find, but the models certainly stand out!

A BRIEF HISTORY OF FLUFF IN AMERICA

By 1917, American confectioner Archibald Query had figured out how to make marshmallows even easier to consume and was hawking Fluff door to door. While he could make the Fluff, he couldn't move it, so he sold the formula to H. Allen Durkee and Fred L. Mower in 1920. They, too, peddled door to door for a while, but did it so well that jars of Fluff soon appeared on grocery shelves. They bought a factory, they hired employees, they automated production, they expanded. Notably, in 1930 Durkee-Mower sponsored a series of fifteen-minute radio shows called "Flufferettes" that were broadcast across New England. In 1947 they redesigned the Fluff jar based on solicited input from customers across America—this same design is used to this day. In 1956 Fluff coproduced a quick and dirty fudge recipe with Nestle. Ten years later the Rice Krispie treat was born. For a specialized, seemingly niche product, Fluff has continued to expand and innovate as a classic American success story. Vive le Fluff!

STAYING POWER

IF THERE WAS A CONTEST for Most Demanding and Grossly Primal Competition, an endurance contest would win. Americans embraced the endurance crazes of the 1920s, and promptly thrust them in the limelight. Whether dancing, or talking, or walking, these contests demanded extremes from the contestants and, almost invariably, turned into wrenching showcases of the breadth of emotion. Contestants became poster children for determination, and desperation. Victories were hard won, and failures were devastating. Though prizes lay at the end of the slog, the distressing, triumphant journeys were hawked as entertainment and gobbled up as inspiration.

HUNKERIN'

ROCKING CHAIR DERBIES

HANDS ON A HARDBODY

NOUN AND VERB RODEO

DANCE MARATHONS

DANCE MARATHONS (CONTINUED)

DANCE MARATHONS (AND CONTINUED!)

HUNKERIN'

THOUGH IT WASN'T *TECHNICALLY* COMPETITIVE, hunkerin' turned out to be a fad that tired out everyone. In the spring of 1959, college campuses were peppered with excitable young people cramming themselves into phone booths, VW beetles, and outhouses. Wide-eyed students getting as close as possible while taking up as little space as possible, well, that was guaranteed entertainment. Fast forward to the fall semester and a very different craze. Apparently the University of Arkansas's Sigma Chi fraternity had a chair deficit, so the brothers opted to squat on their haunches. Everywhere. That's right, they squatted. For whatever reason, this petulant behavior infected the rest of the campus and then spread to others in the South. Soon students were squatting—seriously, sitting on their heels; don't overthink it—all over town. Young people were hunkerin' inside, they were hunkerin' outside! *LIFE Magazine* ran an article, "A Hankerin' for Hunkerin'" in mid-November, 1959, thrusting the hunkerin' mania off the college green. It was reported that students would hunker in groups and do things like discuss politics or sports. But the frat boys' knee-jerk reaction of knee-bending action wasn't really a protest, and it didn't spur any social action. It was just . . . squatting.

Coal City, West Virginia, was no stranger to hunkerin'. Theirs was a circumstantial hunker, however, as many pictured here are coal miners who are used to stooping in the low-ceilinged mines.

ROCKING CHAIR DERBIES

ROCKING CHAIRS WERE A FIXTURE IN AMERICA even before the Declaration of Independence. So why did it take us until the late 1920s to use them competitively?! The few halcyon months before the October 24, 1929, Stock Market Crash became the golden age of the rocker. People were rabid for fads and, on the eve of the crippling Depression, presciently excited about fads that took (wasted, in some cases) the most amount of time without requiring money, or an intense engagement with the world around them—see-saw marathons, months-long tree sitting, the boys who spent sixteen days breaking the longest handshake record without bothering to check if there was a record to break. Chicago residents took to their rockers in late August 1929 in an effort to take down the New York City record of 331 hours of continuous rocking, flocking to the city armed with their own rigs (um, rocking chairs). The New York record remained unbroken, however, leaving Chicago residents less than a month of leisure to console themselves before their Roaring Twenties came crashing down. The marathoning itch had taken hold, though. And as the following Depression decade saw Americans returning to their rockers for more meditative pursuits, the lust for long-term record breaking had been awakened.

This progressive farmer takes a moment to enter, and win, his own derby.

FAMOUS TRAGIC ROCKERS

Americans are no strangers to conspiracy theories and freaky occurrences . . . so here's another!

Abraham Lincoln loved his rocking chair and would request it after particularly long days. One such day was the Friday night he went to Ford's theatre for the last play he'd ever see. John Wilkes Booth (b. 1838) shot Lincoln, shouted *sic semper tyrannis*, and escaped to the Garrett's barn. Subsequently, Andrew Johnson became president.

John F. Kennedy loved his rocking chair and would take it with him everywhere (even Air Force One). On a sunny Friday in 1963, his motorcade wended its way through the streets of Dallas, Texas. Lee Harvey Oswald (b. 1939) shot JFK (though it is the subject of many a theory) from a downtown book depository. Subsequently, Lyndon Johnson became president.

HANDS ON A HARDBODY

IN 1985 A DEALERSHIP IN TEXAS HELD A CONTEST FOR A NISSAN HARDBODY with a deceptively simple premise: to win it, just keep touching the car. As with most endurance competitions, there were regularly scheduled tiny reprieves to give contestants a chance to sit, eat, and use the restroom. These breaks are amazingly effective at ushering in second, third, and further winds, ensuring the contests go on. And on. And on. But the structure of Touch the Truck—or hatchback, or wagon, or sedan—is, conceptually, among the most elegant for competitions: The person who wants the prize the most holds onto the prize the longest, and then gets to keep it. But this concentrated test of will proves why endurance contests should not be taken lightly: Both the losers *and* winners have been led away displaying severe paranoia, rivalry, and psychosis. The 1997 documentary *Hands on a Hardbody* showed the dark side of the competition. This particular brand of endurance contest elicits an intensely emotional response in the entrants, yet the world can't tear its eyes away. The Touch the Truck model is still used today, but many dealerships have come to terms with the price people are paying, and usually give them at least a BMW.

The allure of the car draws a cabal of contestants; let's see who can HANDle it.

HARDBODY TRAGEDY

The contest-originating dealership held its final event in 2005 when one of the more determined contestants suddenly, inexplicably removed his hand from the truck and, in an evident state of distress, crossed the street, bought a gun, and ended his life. Between the darkness documented in the *Hands on a Hardbody* film and the horrible turn of events in 2005, the competition has become more closely associated with mania and desperation than with cars. But the tragedy and weirdness that *Hands on a Hardbody* conjured remains compelling. It has since been turned into a Broadway musical and was rumored to have been a potential project of director Robert Altman when he died.

NOUN AND VERB RODEO

CHRISTMAS DAY, 1928.

71st Regiment Armory.

Twenty-four men.

Eleven women.

Nonstop talking for 23½ out of 24 hours per day.

Profanity disqualifies.

Last one standing after 96 hours wins $1,000.

Three contestants were eliminated almost immediately due to a need for lozenges and a lack of things to say. Hardly anyone in New York City attended the event except for reporters, one of whom described that first day as "thirty-two endings of depressing American novels on show in a ring." The Noun and Verb Rodeo tested the mental, oral, and dental endurance of the contestants, and the patience of the promoter who, by the end of the nearly spectator-less contest, lost more than $10,000 and had the gall to refuse to pay out the prize money. He even stopped the event fifteen minutes before the scheduled finish with no winner being declared. The chattering contestants? Oh, they did not disappoint: One recited Lady Macbeth's speech on a loop until she passed out, while another had to use her words to reject the marriage proposal from a fellow contestant who was then himself disqualified. Ultimately no one won, or made money. Or learned their lesson. One of the two final contestants resumed a healthy career in flagpole sitting, and the promoter went on to host a failed dance marathon in Philadelphia. Only the reporters, with their eagerness to devote ink and brain power to lampooning the rodeo disaster, even after it ended in ignominy, showed they were willing to go the distance.

Delivery and gusto aside, Sirfessor Wilkesbarr's heart wasn't in it and was felled by the rodeo.

LENGTH BREEDS DURATION

Were the Noun and Verb Rodeo to be held today, a contestant could generate a wealth of material by simply reciting a loop with the longest word in English, pneumonoultramicroscopicsilicovolcanoconiosis (a lung disease caused by inhaling volcanic ash); the German entry, Donaudampfschifffahrtsgesellschaftskapitaenswitwe (widow of a Danube steamboat captain); and one from Spain, Esternocleidooccipitomastoideos (a muscle in the neck). For guaranteed hours' worth of speaking, though, one need only invoke the scientific name for titin (the longest protein chain in the human body); with 189,819 letters in it, the word takes around three and a half hours to correctly pronounce.

DANCE MARATHONS

SOME REPORT THAT THE FIRST DANCE MARATHON OCCURRED IN BUTTE, MONTANA, IN 1907. Others, that it was an import in the early 1920s and only really caught on after Europeans started setting and breaking records, bringing Americans' competitiveness bubbling to the surface. But by the late 1920s the marathons were drawing crowds of 20,000-plus during peak hours. With their rise in popularity, the marathons were also coming under increasing scrutiny as contestants were showing signs of acute mental distress at an increasingly alarming rate. Entire cities began imposing time limits on the events and eventually banning them altogether. But just as the future of the event that Americans just couldn't look away from was being called into question, the nation entered the Great Depression. America's leanest hour turned out to be just the boon that marathon promoters needed: People were desperate for money, so there was never a want for entrants, and everyone else was desperate for schadenfreude, so there was never a want for fascinated onlookers. "Dance marathons" had a tainted reputation, but their identical cousin, "walkathons," were embraced by communities, which would set up camp for weeks at a time to test entrants' limits, and then some.

STANDARD DANCE MARATHON RULES

Dancers must remain dancing at all times. Shuffling back and forth is acceptable, but if a dancer's knees hit the floor he or she is eliminated.

Dancers will remain on the dance floor at all times when not on break.

Dancers may compete alone, or in pairs, but if one-half of the pair is eliminated, the remaining dancer must find a new partner in twenty-four hours or be eliminated.

Dancers will perform the prescribed dances for the appropriate songs (e.g., Charleston, foxtrot, tango).

A five- to fifteen-minute break is given every hour, at which time dancers will retire to an area with cots.

If a dancer falls asleep he or she must stay upright; the dancer may be supported by his or her partner as long as neither's knees hit the floor.

Meals and toileting are to be done off the floor.

Dancers will always look presentable: Women will wear skirts except in the early morning hours, and men will wear shirts and collars.

Dancers will behave with decorum: Spitting, chewing gum, profanity, and fighting will result in elimination.

Looks fun, doesn't it?

DANCE MARATHONS (CONTINUED)

THE GREAT DEPRESSION BRED DESPERATION IN AMERICA. Dance marathons theoretically relieved that by giving the dancers guaranteed shelter and food, and the audience members an outlet for their anger and newfound sense of inferiority. The marathons were spectacles that America could not look away from. Naturally, promoters began doubling-down on their investments in the name of box office receipts. First, it was more common than not for the marathons to be peppered with professionals—people who knew how to navigate the insular marathon world—who would keep the contest moving along while representing a standard against which amateurs' failures could be visibly measured. Second, the promoters would raise the stakes. Elimination events were generally instituted after the first one hundred hours of dancing, and they were guaranteed audience pleasers, as these trials were seriously, cruelly demanding. But pain and failure were surefire moneymakers.

The hours, days, and weeks wear on.

ELIMINATION HEAT SCHEDULE

MONDAY: Zombie Treadmills, one hour. (These events were heavily promoted and heavily attended, as it meant blindfolding both dancers as a couple, tying an end of a rope to each of them, then having them race.)

TUESDAY: Figure-Eight Races, twenty-five laps.

WEDNESDAY: Elimination Lap Races—male contestants.

THURSDAY: Dynamite Sprints.

FRIDAY: Heel and Toe Derbies. (Dancers had to dance on just their heels or just their tippy toes for as long as possible.)

SATURDAY: Elimination Lap Races—female contestants.

GRINDS TO FOLLOW.

CONTINUOUS DANCING. No breaks. Couples are only relieved when one collapses.

DANCE MARATHONS (AND CONTINUED!)

BUT EVEN OVER-THE-TOP PHYSICAL TRIALS DIDN'T WORK to thin the pack every time. As these events could literally last for months, the promoters worked with the emcee to hone in on and exploit any interpersonal drama between the dancers. There were rivalries, romances, betrayals—the works! The bosses would pull out all the stops to keep the audience guessing, and coming back for more. Like the marathon in Spokane, Washington, featuring the "Grand Public Wedding of the Ohio Sweetheart Team. . . . The wedding of Florence Ollie and Jack Stanley, Couple 22, will take place on the Walkathon Floor amidst all the remaining contestants as attendants." And if that didn't work, there was a veteran marathoner who was famous for being "frozen in ice" twice a day, dancing without moving any part of his body beyond his feet. The dancers had an intense pressure to perform, and a whole litany of rules to follow, but the bosses generally only obeyed the almighty dollar.

The desperation that the marathons both abused and engendered started to outweigh the spectacle in the mid-1930s. Towns across the country were banning the marathons, and people started seeing them as a form of slow torture. The prizes were less appealing when physical and mental well-being were on the line.

By the end of the mania, the marathon record that had been set was so extreme, and set under such extreme circumstances, that it stands to this day.

5,152 hours = 7 months, 2 days
August 29, 1930 through April 1, 1931
Mike Ritof and Edith Boudreaux
$2,000 (about $30,000 in 2016 dollars)
Chicago, Illinois

Dance partners supported each other, in every way.

AMATEUR MAGICIANS CONTEST
TRICKS • NOVEL ENTERTAINMENT• JUGGLERS • SHADOWGRAPHY• MIMICS ETC. ALL BOYS AND GIRLS ARE ELIGIBLE. REGISTER AT YOUR PLAYGROUND NOW.
CONDUCTED BY THE PARKS MAGIC MAN
TUES. SEPT. 8 AT 2:30 P.M.
ROOSEVELT PLAYGROUND
DEPARTMENT OF PARKS
USA WORK WPA

ACKNOWLEDGMENTS

I went to a party and got drunk one night in college. It wasn't until the following morning that I realized I had committed a dreaded pocket dial in the hazy wee hours. As my mother was not awake to answer it, the call went to voicemail on her phone. Stuff of nightmares, right? The message was upward of six minutes long—six minutes I definitely didn't remember. She called me later in the day to address the voicemail antics. With shaky breath and clammy hands, I steeled myself for the worst.

Apparently, even in a college-fueled stupor, I couldn't help myself from singing Mom's praises. "I looooove my mom," I asserted over the giggles and chatter of the party. "No. Really. She's great. Really. I looooooove my mom." To her credit, Mom seemed appropriately flattered, and horrified. We laughed about it and then quickly moved on. Honestly, though: no regrets. I'd do it again in a second. I loooooove my mom.

An acknowledgment is a big deal.

A drunken voicemail is the tops, though.

Let's not be cocky, though; there are loads of folks I'm unapologetically grateful for:

Tim, my favorite falconer.

Clara, my iron-willed inspiration.

Gwen, my hero, and heroine.

Keith, the supportive, whip-smart guy who took a chance on my words.

Juli, who saved me.

Walter, who I miss lots and lots.

Stella, who is so beautiful, and so dumb.

Popo, who can't seem to behave himself.

Rachel, because I love my mom.

And, truly, David Lynch, Steve Carrell, Matt Groening, Billy Wilder, Billy West, Chihiro, Werner Herzog, Ripley and Jones, Tony Perkins, Beetlejuice, and Dorothy Michaels—I'd be lost without you.

GRAND CHAMPION

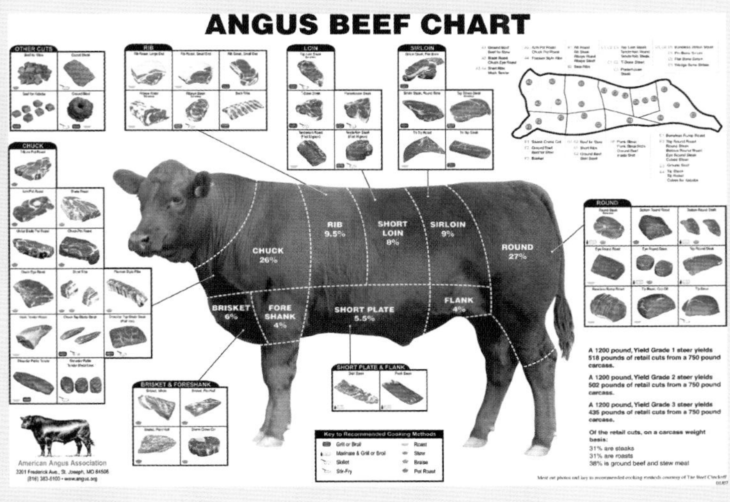
ANGUS BEEF CHART
OTHER CUTS
RIB
LOIN
SIRLOIN
CHUCK
ROUND
BRISKET & FORESHANK
SHORT PLATE & FLANK
CHUCK 26%
RIB 9.5%
SHORT LOIN 8%
SIRLOIN 9%
ROUND 27%
BRISKET 6%
FORE SHANK 4%
SHORT PLATE 5.5%
FLANK 4%
A 1200 pound, Yield Grade 1 steer yields 518 pounds of retail cuts from a 750 pound carcass.
A 1200 pound, Yield Grade 2 steer yields 502 pounds of retail cuts from a 750 pound carcass.
A 1200 pound, Yield Grade 3 steer yields 435 pounds of retail cuts from a 750 pound carcass.
Of the retail cuts, on a carcass weight basis:
31% are steaks
31% are roasts
38% is ground beef and stew meat
Key to Recommended Cooking Methods
Grill or Broil
Marinate & Grill or Broil
Skillet
Stir-Fry
Roast
Stew
Braise
Pot Roast
American Angus Association
3201 Frederick Ave., St. Joseph, MO 64506
(816) 383-5100 • www.angus.org

PHOTO CREDITS

4: heads-down pie-eating—Library of Congress

5: Diving into victory—DC VegFest Cupcake Eating Contest © Compassion Over Killing (https://www.flickr.com/photos/tryveg/8026930258/)

8–11: istock.com

9: Alvin "Shipwreck" Kelly—AP Photo

12–13: Doughnuts—Library of Congress; Tug of War—US National Archives; Ribbons—Library of Congress; Grow it—Library of Congress; Fluff hair—©Union Square Main Streets

INTRODUCTION

14. Pink pageant—Working in Paterson Project Collection (AFC 1995/028), Library of Congress

15. Eating contest—Library of Congress; Greased pig—US National Archives

16. Rodeo mascot—Library of Congress

ON YOUR MARKS

Boom Run

21. Leaping from log to log—Boom run competitor at Lake Wingra - Madison WI - 06-28-2015 2820 © Richard Hurd (https://www.flickr.com/photos/rahimageworks/19255778815/in/album-72157634407752555/). CC BY 2.0

Lawn Mower Racing

23. STA-BIL red mowers—Courtesy of the USLMRA; yellow and green mowers—Courtesy of NASGRASS Inc.

The Great Bunion Derby

25. Andy Payne, who will go on to win the race—NatPar Collection/Alamy Stock Photo; Bed of Nails—Bed of Nails © fabian .kron (https://www.flickr.com/photos/mrdoctor/15781343203). CC BY-ND 2.0

Bed Racing

27. With tissue paper tiki torches—SAU Family Day 13 Bed Races_9032 © Southern Arkansas University (https://www.flickr.com/photos/saumag/9938707873/in/album-72157635889206216/). CC BY 2.0

Six Day Bicycle Races

29. The second iteration of Madison Square Garden—George Grantham Bain Collection, Library of Congress; Even when essentially empty—George Grantham Bain Collection, Library of Congress

Shovel Racing

31. Outstanding form—Angel Fire Shovel Races 2011 © Lynn Eubank (https://c2.staticflickr.com/6/5011/5446737522_ca00fc8e2b_o.jpg). CC BY-NC-SA 2.0; Not so outstanding form— "Angel Fire Shovel Races 2011" © Lynn Eubank (https://www.flickr.com/photos/lynneubank/5446738666/)

Joggling

33. Rumor has it he dropped the balls— Stranger #3 © Phil Roeder (https://www.flickr.com/photos/tabor-roeder/5073055809/in/photolist-8JhJKt). CC BY 2.0; U.S. Coast Guard Academy Third Class Cadet—Petty Officer NyxoLyno Cangemi, US Coast Guard Academy

24 Hours of LeMons

35. A parade of speeding misfits—"24 Hours of LeMons-Sonoma Raceway, December 2013" © Brian Shamblen (https://www.flickr.com/photos/23972840@N04/11282450764/)

Outhouse Racing

37. Even South Haven, Michigan, gets into the potty—AP Photo/The Herald-Palladium, Don Campbell

Redneck Blank, Pig Roast and Music Festival

39. Joe "Nailbender" Pike dives—AP Photo/Erik S. Lesser

HERE SHE IS . . .

Miss America

42. What's better than a beauty queen in a bathing costume?—Venice Bathing Beauty Pageant, 1926, Library of Congress

43. Looking bored and beautiful—Library of Congress

Harvest Queen

45. A portrait of the Queen—National Archives; The winners of the Thanksgiving Day beauty pageant—both National Archives

Miss Unsafe Brakes

47. Sexy and informative—Courtesy of the Chicago Auto Show

Miss'd America

49. Big, and bright, and colorful, drag queen beauty pageants—2008 Universal ShowQueen Pageant © Hawaiian Moore (https://www.flickr.com/photos/moorealoha/2607944363)

Miss Klingon Empire

51. Though only one walks away victorious—"IMG_5509" © Hillary (https://www.flickr.com/photos/lamenta3/3943632170/in/album-72157622429437000/)

QUESTIONABLE FUN AND ESTEEMED TITLES

Mr. Mosquito Legs

55. Willie Man Chew Sees All—© Arthur Forman

Little Mr. Chaos and Miss Miscellaneous

57. No word on whether prizes are awarded—Public Domain

The Hatfield McCoy Marathon & The Tug Fork Tug of War

59. This thar winner—AP Photo/*Williamson Daily News*, Kyle Lovern

World Pillow Fight Championship

61. When good pillows go bad—"DSC09227" © Matthew Simantov (https://www.flickr.com/photos/msimdottv/3438200315) CC BY 2.0; The inauspicious origins—"Once over!" © Library and Archives Canada (https://www.flickr.com/photos/lac-bac/5084701948) CC BY 2.0

Coffin Race Championship

63. Alive and well—Rex Features via AP Images

Worm Gruntin' Championship

65. A beauty queen—AP Photo/Phil Coale

Disc Golf Championship

67.Headless, and proud—Photos courtesy Fruita Parks and Recreation; Disc Golf is for birds of all feathers "bluebird mom ready to play disc golf dunham june 2013" ©ptgbirdlover (https://www.flickr.com/photos/peapod51/9013113905/sizes/o/) CC BY 2.0; (kid throwing

frisbee)—"Gabe Playing Disc Golf" © Jon Rogers (https://www.flickr.com/photos/jonmrogers/5895111791/)

The Undie 500

69. "But it is not a race" © Lars Plougmann (https://www.flickr.com/photos/criminalintent/5963258584)

FESTS AND CONTESTS

Bubble Gum Blowing

73. A strong jaw—AP Photo/Charlie Neibergall

Kcymaerxthaere Spelling Bee

75. Spelling is hard—Harris and Ewing Collection, Library of Congress

Moo-la-Palooza

77. To achieve victory—Public Domain; Mooed out—"let sleeping cows lie" © Bryan Ledgard (https://www.flickr.com/photos/ledgard/2146739834/)

Rotten Sneaker Contest

78. Montpelier, Vermont, is where, once a year—AP Photo/Toby Talbot

79. The Godfather of athletic wear—Chuck Taylor © Schroder+Schombs PR (https://www.flickr.com/photos/schroederschoembs/2415285753)

Super Farmer Contest

81. The county fair in Leesburg, Virginia, tests—Hay bale toss © Jason McKnight (https://www.flickr.com/photos/fullyum/20047160060/in/photolist m2r9J-wxuWfG-2TodMQ-2TocnC-2Tog1C-a432bS-m2qSL). CC BY 2.0

The Great Salt Lick Contest

83. Abstract. Postmodern. Cubist. Salty—"Salt Lick Art" © Alan Davey (https://www.flickr.com/photos/adavey/3830075093) CC BY 2

Milk Chugging Contest

85. The 2014 Legislative Milk-Chugging contest—Courtesy N.C. Department of Agriculture and Consumer Services

Mom and Husband Calling

87. Volume. Insistence. Threats—Courtesy of Leann and Rex Hewitt

Ladies' Rubber Chicken Throwing Contest

89. Pick a little, peck a little—Iowa State Fair; The 1981 bench for Stroud, Oklahoma—Patrick Ward/Alamy Stock Photo

Decorated Diaper Contest and Diaper Derby

91. Competition is tough—Ready, set, go © Quinn Dombrowski (https://www.flickr.com/photos/quinnanya/11150887605/).CC BY-SA 2.0

DERBY, OR NOT DERBY?

Dole Air Derby

95. A successful takeoff—"Dole Air Race Breese" Pabco Pacific Flyer "NX646" © SDASM Archives (https://www.flickr.com/photos/sdasmarchives/8091673071/); One unlucky entrant—"AL-47 Olseon Album Image_000059" © SDASM Archives (https://www.flickr.com/photos/sdasmarchives/13472194315/)

All-American Soap Box Derby

97. Jimmy, looking happy with his trophy—AP Photo/Steve Pyle; Speed demons—"DSC_1138_pp" © Walter (https://www.flickr.com/photos/walterpro/15442666605/)

Father's Day Fishing Derby

99. The early fisherman—AP Photo/Alden Pellett; SEE IT?!—"Puget Sound Sea Serpent" © Cliff (https://www.flickr.com/photos/fishingwithcliff/2214535748/)

All-American Dog Derby

101. YIP/BARK/WOOF/MUSH—AP Photo/The *Idaho Post-Register*, Robert Bower; There's no telling who's mushing—Public Domain, via Wikimedia Commons

The Kentucky Derby

103. These horses were born to be blurry. —"Kentucky Derby 2014-0214" © Bill Brine (https://www.flickr.com/photos/8099556@N08/14130332164/); Even while practicing, Secretariat—AP Photo

Roller Derby

105. A derby girl—*New York World-Telegram and Sun* Newspaper Photograph Collection, Library of Congress

Demolition Derbies and Destructive Motorsports

107. Amidst the dust—"DuPage County Demolition Derby" © Daniel X. O'Neil (https://www.flickr.com/photos/juggernautco/6001227683)

NO THANKS, I'M STUFFED!

Goldfish Swallowing

111. An ill-advised pastime—AP Photo

Pie Eating Contests

113. Vintage mmmmmmmmmm—both Library of Congress; Eat! Eat! Eat!—Weight-Loss Ad (FDA154) © The U.S. Food and Drug Administration (https://www.flickr.com/photos/fdaphotos/8212182572/)

Nathan's Famous Hot Dog Eating Contest

115. Patrick "Deep Dish" Bertoletti—img_3422 © Michael (https://www.flickr.com/photos/helloturkeytoe/4762327028/in/photostream/); Puns make everything taste better—© Paul Brennan

The Manhattan Fat Men's Club

117. As if we needed someone to spell it out—Library of Congress; Little Big Joe Cody—Library of Congress

Alferd Packer Day Snacker Contest

119. Packer before prison and after prison—both Public Domain

MoonPie Eating Contests

121. Moon pie—"Moon Pie" © JD Hancock (https://www.flickr.com/photos/jdhancock/3658631267); Horace Fletcher—Fornier, Paul, photographer. [Horace Fletcher, half-length portrait, facing slightly right]. September 14, ca. 1908. Image. Retrieved from the Library of Congress, (https://www.loc.gov/item/2004671581/)

Cupcake Chomping Contests

123. Diving into victory—DC VegFest Cupcake Eating Contest © Compassion Over Killing (https://www.flickr.com/photos/tryveg/8026930258/)

La Costeña Feel the Heat Jalapeño Eating Contest

125. While most people would give these peppers a wide berth—AP Photo/Walla Walla Union-Bulletin, Greg Lehman

The Ill-advised, the Unconventional, and the Unfortunate

127. It looks like the onlookers are having a great time!—"Pickled egg eating contest in the Legion Hall, Cadomin, Alberta" © Provincial Archives of Alberta (https://www.flickr.com/photos/alberta_archives/25938555971)

BECAUSE, WHY NOT?

Phone Booth Stuffing

131. Looks comfy, no?—AP Photo

Flagpole Sitting

133. A clown on a flagpole. Seriously—AP Photo

Kissing Contests

135. Lip-locking in 1998—Marty Lederhandler/AP

Rock, Paper, Scissors!

137. Tension runs high—AP Photo/Jae C. Hong; Even in its infant days—Documerica, The U.S. National Archives

Ugly Lamp Contest

138. Kentucky State Fair, 1999—AP Photo/Brian Bohannon

139. In the wild the lamps—Ugly Lamp © rreihm (https://www.flickr.com/photos/backorder/4922474680). CC BY 2.0

Ugly Dog Contest

141. A face that only a mother—AP Photo/Noah Berger

Horse Soccer

143. It takes time for horses to get used to the giant ball—IMG_2284.jpg © John Ramspott (https://www.flickr.com/photos/jramspott/4872104955/in/album-72157624556328445/) CC BY 2.0; Now we're showing that ball who's boss!—IMG_2297.jpg © John Ramspott (https://www.flickr.com/photos/jramspott/4872716622/sizes/o/) CC BY 2.0

Turkey Bowling

145. Throwing frozen [wish]bones—AP Photo/Morning Sentinel, Jonathan Adams; Pardoned and ready to fly the coop!—Reagan Library, C43795-20

Most Gifted Wrapper

147. A finalist wends and wraps—Courtesy of SCOTCH BRAND/ Ray Stubblebine

Duct Tape Prom Dresses!

149. 2014 finalists in what was, undoubtedly, a sticky competition—Rex Features via AP Images

HARDER, BETTER, FASTER, STRONGER

Venus de Milo Lookalike

153. (Unrealistic beauty standards—Clarence H. White, Library of Congress; The Wellesley Thoracimeter—George Grantham Bain Collection, Library of Congress

Livestock Showcase

155. Pride and solemnity at the 4H fair—Cow Proud © Nathan Siemers (https://www.flickr.com/photos/nosha/4310660773); Forth Worth, Texas, 1959—Grand Champion Steer, Ft. Worth, 1959, photograph, Date Unknown, (texashistory.unt.edu/ark:/67531/metapth43968/m1/1/: accessed March 27, 2017), University of North Texas Libraries, The Portal to Texas History, texashistory.unt.edu; crediting Cattle Raisers Museum

Agricultural Royalty

157. They truly had it all...—"Miss Stock Grower," Connie Blake, Nebraska Stock Growers Association, The Beef State, Bassett, Nebraska; and 1968's Miss Nebraska Stock Grower, Ann Coffee, Harrison, Nebraska, Convention Queen of the Meat Meet; Without the inventions—Lewis Hine, National Archives

America's Giant Produce!

159. The cabbage weigh-off winners—Courtesy Clark James Mishler/Courtesy of Alaska State Fair; (The reindeer is for scale!)—Courtesy Clark James Mishler/Courtesy of Alaska State Fair

Bingo (Cow Chip, or Chicken)

161. This chick is ready—© Sarah G (https://www.flickr.com/photos/fat_tony/2837774315/)

Watermelon Pitted Against Watermelon

162. Picture perfect seed spittin'—© CampJoyOhio (https://commons.wikimedia.org/wiki/File:Seed-Spitting_@_Program_Building.jpg)

163. Prepped to roll to victory—*New York World-Telegram and Sun* Newspaper Photograph Collection, Library of Congress

The Mystic Krewe of Barkus

165. A little pooch in his barkus box—Krewe of Barkus and Meoux Pet Parade, Shreveport, LA © Shreveport-Bossier Convention and Tourist Bureau (https://www.flickr.com/photos/shreveportbossier/8445286437/); Smiling parade pit—Krewe of Barkus and Meoux Pet Parade, Shreveport, LA © Shreveport-Bossier Convention and Tourist Bureau (https://www.flickr.com/photos/shreveportbossier/8445286437/)

POTLUCK!

Morel Pole–National Morel Mushroom Festival

169. A GIANT DELICACY— "Deb found this morel in May 2009" © Deb Deppeler (https://www.flickr.com/photos/debdep/3527976299/)

Great Garlic Cook-Off—Gilroy Garlic Festival

171. Herbie, the head of garlic—Bill Strange, courtesy of Gilroy Garlic Festival Association, Inc.; Garlic, anthropomorphized, and enlarged—© Hydrargyrum (https://en.wikipedia.org/wiki/File:Gilroy_Garlic_Festival_2010_inflatable.jpg)

Frog Leg Festival

173. Where the magic happens...—Courtesy of the Fellsmere Frog Leg Festival; The "before" photo—Courtesy of the Fellsmere Frog Leg Festival

Blue Ribbon Cricket Eating Contest

175. Edible? Check. Appetizing? Eh...—"On a plate—Fried Giant Water Bug..." © Alpha (https://www.flickr.com/photos/avlxyz/3429008880/)

Cabbage Bowling, Toss, Decorating, Beer—Sauerkraut Weekend

177. It's hard to say if a pin is worth more—Photo courtesy of VisitFingerLakes.com

West Virginia Roadkill Cook-Off & Autumn Harvest Festival

179. BON APPETIT.—"roadkill cafe" © Greg Habermann (https://www.flickr.com/photos/smomashup1/5947935675/); Always look both ways before crossing the street—AP Photo /News & Record, Nelson Kepley; Rules for camel roadkill are unclear...—AP Photo

Great Potato Cook-Off—Barnesville Potato Days

181. Before the sport matured into mashed tater wrestlin'—Lee Russell, Library of Congress

Fluff Cooking Contest—What the Fluff! Festival

183. A Fluff official with bags of Fluff—"Fluff Fest 2012" © Todd van Hoosear (https://www.flickr.com/photos/vanhoosear/8039183361/); Fluff stylists are hard to find—© Union Square Main Streets

STAYING POWER

Hunkerin'

187. Coal City, West Virginia, was no stranger to hunkerin'—DOCUMERICA: The Environmental Protection Agency's Program to Photographically Document Subjects of Environmental Concern, 1972–1977, The National Archives

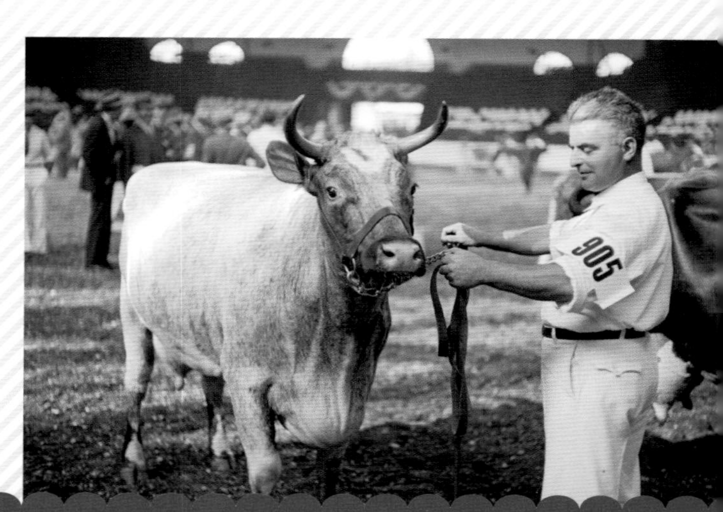

Rocking Chair Derbies

189. This progressive farmer—"Farmer Reading his Farm Paper" by George W. Ackerman, 1931

Hands on a Hardbody

191. The allure of the car—Imaginechina via AP Images

Noun and Verb Rodeo

193. Delivery and gusto aside, Sirfessor Wilkesbarr's heart wasn't in it—From the archives of Kevin I. Slaughter of unionofegoists.com

Dance Marathons

195. Looks fun, doesn't it?—Library of Congress Prints and Photographs Division

Dance Marathons *(Continued)*

197. The hours, days, and weeks wear on—Heritage Image Partnership Ltd / Alamy Stock Photo

Dance Marathons *(and Continued!)*

199. Dance partners supported each other, in every way—Sueddeutsche Zeitung Photo / Alamy Stock Photo

200–201. Diving—Library of Congress; Pipe Smoking—Farm Security Administration, New York Public Library; Magicians poster—Library of Congress; Trophy in hand—Library of Congress; Artillery horses—Yale University Library; Typewriters—Library of Congress

Acknowledgments. Calling—All Library of Congress

204–205. Pies—US National Archives; Rope—US National Archives; Swim trophy—Library of Congress; Rabbit—Library of Congress; Beef chart—American Angus Association; Children art—US National Archives; Horseshoe pitching—Library of Congress

Photo Credits section. Trophy dog—"2009 Big Bay Balloon Parade" © Dale Frost (http://www.flickr.com/photos/portofsandiego/4228800705) CC by 2.0; Wheelbarrows—US National Archives; Fiddlers—US National Archives; Fish—US National Archives; Women lineup—US National Archives; Roping competition—Library of Congress; Diving—Library of Congress; Dairy Competition—Library of Congress

Index. Model airplanes—Library of Congress; Dance contest—Library of Congress; Barrel rolling—Library of Congress; Ice skating—Library of Congress; Oxen—Library of Congress

About the Author. Fuzzy bridesmaid and leering pig—Rachel Dickinson; leopard print and kitty belly—Gwendolyn Gallagher; all others by the author

INDEX

AASBD (All-American Soap Box Derby), 96–97
acorns, 169
advertisements, 46–47
agricultural royalty, 156–57
air flight derby, 93–95
Alferd Packer Snacker Contest, 118–19
All-American Dog Derby, 100–101
All-American Soap Box Derby (AASBD), 96–97
Angel Fire Resort, 30–31
automobile endurance races, 34–35

Barnesville Potato Days, 180–81
Barr, Roseanne, 81
bathing costumes, 42–43
beauty pageants
about, 40–41
bed racing, 26–27
Bertoletti, Patrick "Deep Dish," 122
bicycle races, 28–29
bingo, 160–61
black walnuts, 169
Blue Ribbon Cricket Eating Contest, 174–75
boom runs, 20–21
bovine impersonators, 76–77
bubble gum blowing, 72–73
Bunion Derby, 24

cabbage contests, 176–77
Cagney, James, 81
cannibals, 118–19
Carl's Jr. commercial, 47
carnivores, 119
Cash, Johnny, 81
chess boxing, 33
Chicago Auto Show, 46–47
chicken chip bingo, 160–61
Christmas presents, 147
Chuck Taylors (sneakers), 79
Cody, Little Big Joe, 117
coffin-race championships, 62–63
collars (high), 149
commercials, 46–47
Converse Rubber Shoe Company, 79
Cook, Captain James, 177
corsets, 149
cow chip bingo, 160–61
cricket eating contests, 174–75
cryogenics, 62–63
cupcake eating contests, 122–23

Dairy Princesses, 156
dance marathons, 194–99
dandelions, 169
Decorated Diaper Derby, 90–91
demolition derbies, 106–7
destructive motorsports, 106–7

detachable high-collars, 149
Diaper Derby, 90–91
Disc Golf Championship, 66–67
Dog Derby, 100–101
dog parades, 164–65
dogsled teams, 100–101
Dole Air Derby, 94–95
drag queen beauty pageants, 48–49
Dubble Bubble, 72
duct tape prom dresses, 148–49

Eeyore's birthday party, 69
The Egg and I, 14–16
elimination schedules for dance marathons, 196–97
Erie County Fair, 17
extreme ironing, 33

Father's Day Fishing Derby, 98–99
Fat Men's Clubs, 116–17
Fellsmere Frog Leg Festival, 172–73
FFA (Future Farmers of America), 154
fictional characters, 13–17
fishing derby, 98–99
flagpole sitting, 132–33
Flathead Lake Monster, 99
Fletcher, Horace, 121
Fluff contests, 182–83
foraging for edibles, 169
4H (Head, Heart, Hands, and Health), 154–55

Franklin, Benjamin, 81
French kissing, 135
Frog Leg Festival, 172–73
Frozen Dead Guy Days, 62–63
Funny Car Drag Racing, 35
Future Farmers of America (FFA), 154

garlic festivals, 170–71
giant produce, 158–59
gift wrapping contests, 146–47
Gila River Internment Camp, 44–45
Gilroy Garlic Festival, 170–71
Golden Mermaid, 42–43
goldfish swallowing, 110–11
Great Bed Races, 27
Great Salt Lick Contest, 82–83
Great Texas Mosquito Festival, 54–55
Gronen, Jimmy, 97
gum blowing, 72–73

Hands on a Hardbody contest, 190–91
Harvest Queen, 44–45
Hatfield McCoy Reunion Festival, 58–59
hollerin' culture, 87
horse races, 102–3
horse soccer, 142–43
Hot Dog Eating Contests, 114–15
hot pepper eating contests, 124–25
hunkerin', 186–87
Husband Calling contest, 86–87

IJA (International Jugglers' Association), 32
insect festivals, 54–55, 174–75
International Jugglers' Association (IJA), 30
inventions, 157
Iowa State Fair, 86–89

Jackass (TV show), 85
Jalapeños Eating Contest, 124–25
Japanese American internment, 44–45
joggling, 32–33
Johnson, Derrick, 144
juggling and jogging, 32–33

Kcymaerxthaere Spelling Bee, 74
Kelly, Alvin "Shipwreck," 132–33
Kennedy, John F., 189
Kentucky Derby, 102–13
Kentucky Derby Festival, 27
kissing contests, 134–35
Klingons, 50–51

La Costena pepper company, 124
Ladies' Rubber Chicken Throwing Contest, 88–89
Las Vegas, 137
lawn mover racing, 22–23
LeMons races, 34–35
Lincoln, Abraham, 189
Little Mister and Miss Chaos, 56
livestock showcases, 154–55
log rolling championships, 20–21
Lowe, Ed, 161
Lumberjack World Championships, 20–21

Mardi Gras, 164–65
Mike, the headless chicken, 66–67
milk chugging contest, 84–85
Miss America, 42–43
Miss and Mr. Miscellaneous, 56
Miss'd America pageant, 48–49
Miss Klingon Empire, 50–51
Miss Unsafe Brakes, 46–47
Mom Calling contest, 86
Moo-la-Palooza, 76–77
MoonPie eating contests, 120–21
morel mushrooms, 168–69
Morstoel, Bredo, 62
mosquito festivals, 54–55
Most Gifted Wrapper contest, 146–47
Mr. Chaos, 56–57
Mr. Mosquito Legs, 54
mushroom contests, 168–69
music festivals, 38–39
Mystic Krewe of Barkus, 164–65

Nathan's Famous Hot Dog Eating Contest, 114–15
National Hollerin' Contest, 87
National Western Stock Show, 154
Nissan commercial, 47
North Carolina milk chugging contest, 84–85
Northeaster Primitive Rendezvous, 69
Noun and Verb Rodeo, 192–93
nuts, 169

Ocean City (New Jersey) contests, 56–57
Odor-Eaters, 78
Olympics (Redneck), 38–39
outhouse racing, 36–37

Packer, Alferd, 118–19
Payne, Andy, 24, 25
Perrier water commercial, 47
phone booth stuffing, 130–31
pie eating contests, 112–13
pig roasts, 38–39
pillow fight championships, 60–61
potato cook-offs, 180–81
produce record holders, 158–59
 See also specific produce
Pyle, C. C., 24

Query, Archibald, 182–83

Redneck Blank, Pig Roast and Music Festival, 38–39
roadkill cook-offs, 178–79
Rock, Paper, Scissors (RPS) sport, 136–37
rocking chair derbies, 188–89
roller derbies, 104–5
Rolling Pin Throwing Contest, 89
Rotten Sneaker Contest, 78
RPS (Rock, Paper, Scissors) sport, 136–37
rubber chicken throwing, 88–89

Sargent, Dudley Allen, 152
Sauerkraut Weekend, 176–77
scandals, 97
Scripps National Spelling Bee, 75
scurvy, 177
sexy ads for unsexy products, 46–47
Sheba cat food commercial, 47
shovel racing, 30–31
Six Days of New York, 28–29
Snacker Contest, 118–19
soccer (horse), 142–43
spelling bees, 74–75
spicy foods, 124–25
squatting, 186–87
Star Trek, 50–51
stationary competition, 25
Stuck at Prom Scholarship Contest, 148–49

Super Farmer contests, 80–81

tapeworm diet, 113
Tarantula Awareness Festival, 69
Testicle Festival (Testy Fest), 68–69
Thanksgiving Day beauty
pageant, 44–45
throwing contests, 88–89
Touch the Truck contest, 190–91
Transcontinental Roller Derby, 104
Triple Crown winners, 103
truffles, 169
Tug Fork tug of war, 58–59
turkey bowling, 144–45

Ugly Dog Contest, 140–41
Ugly Lamp Contest, 138–39
underwater hockey, 33
Undie 500, 68–69
unicycle football, 33
United States Lawn Mower Racing
Association (USLMRA), 22

Venus de Milo Lookalike contest, 152–53

waterbed racing, 27
watermelon records, 162–63
weaponry (otherwise innocuous), 60–61
weight loss, 121
What the Fluff? Festival, 182–83
Whitey, the White River Monster, 99
wild asparagus, 169
Willie Man-Chew, 54–55
World Pillow Fight Championship, 60–61
Worm Gruntin' Championship, 64–65
Wrench Throwing Contest, 89

ABOUT THE AUTHOR

RAILEY JANE SAVAGE is an editor and artist and television enthusiast. She has a strong background in film studies and an expensive English degree from Smith College, which has proven 100% worth the time, money, and agony that comes with a liberal arts degree. Savage loves her family, expects her sisters to take over the world, and lives happily with two ill-behaved cats in Ithaca, New York.